a systematic approach
to behavior management
and positive teaching

People will become better the more they are told how good they really are.

any teacher can...

a systematic approach to behavior management and positive teaching

by Helen Shipman, IBVM and Elizabeth Foley

Loyola University Press

Chicago 60657

LIBRARY OF CONGRESS
CATALOGING IN PUBLICATION DATA

Shipman, Helen, 1938-
  Any teacher can...

  Bibliography: p.
  1. Classroom management.   2. Behaviorism
(Psychology)   I. Foley, Elizabeth, joint author.
II. Title.
LB3011.S486   371.1'02   73-10243
ISBN 0-8294-0220-9

© 1973 Loyola University Press
Printed in the United States of America

Photographs by James Vorwoldt, S.J.

*Read all of
Any Teacher Can.*

, and Tim with
iave teachers
nciples and
know the joy

contents

Foreword — ix

Introduction — 1

1 Positive Teaching — 5

2 Grandma's Law — 19

3 How To Begin — 27

4 Ground Rules — 33

5 A Token Economy — 41

6 Helps for Learning — 51

7 Problems and Discipline — 63

8 Shaping New Behavior — 75

Appendix A The SCAN Plan — 81

Appendix B Cross-level Tutoring — 87

Bibliography — 91

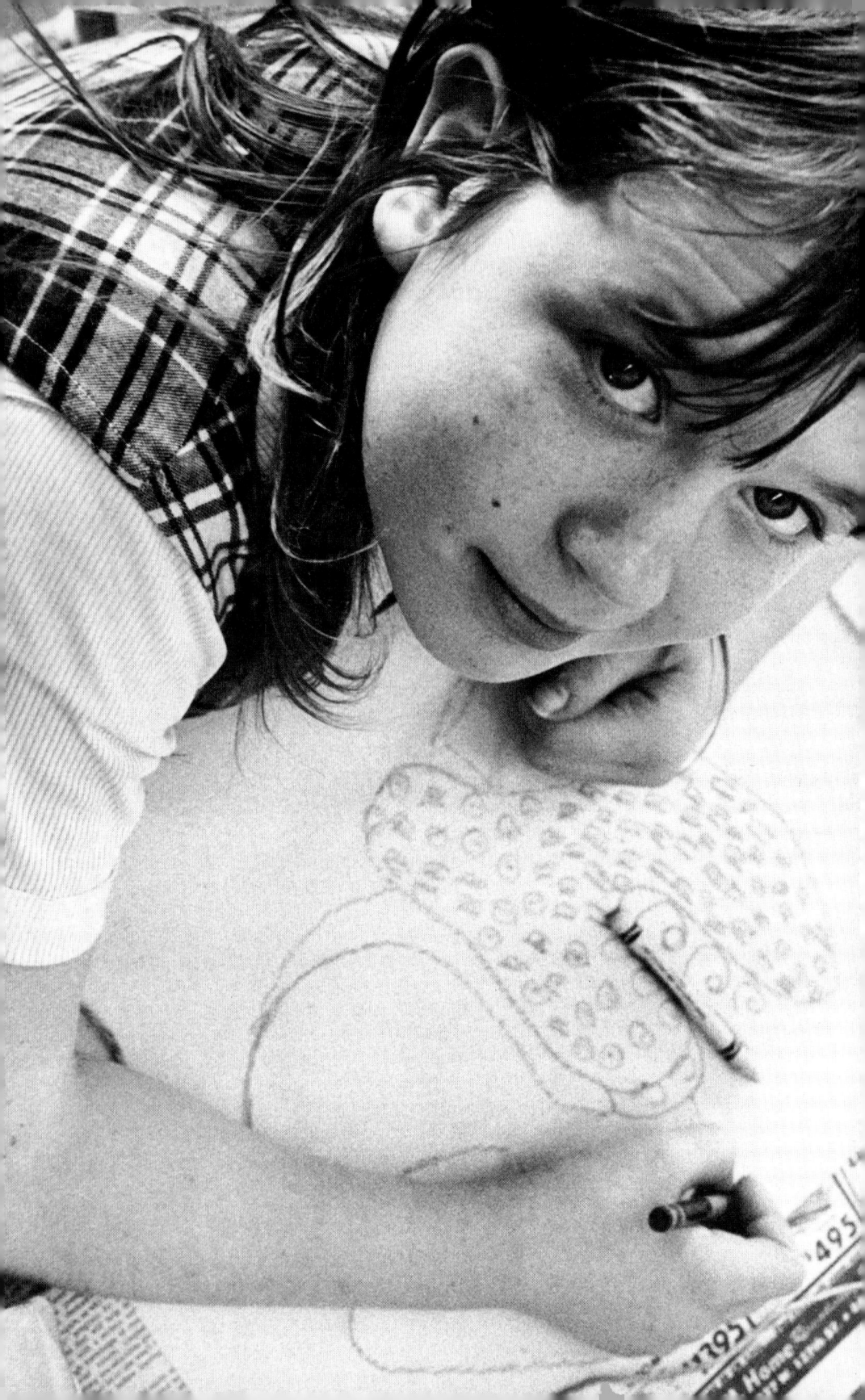

foreword

Human life is like a long river. It begins as a spring, rushes down a mountainside, widens, deepens, matures, and finally flows gently into the ocean.

The newborn baby, like the rivulet, is fresh and pure; both the baby and the stream of water depend on many sources and influences for their growth and direction. Both soon acquire a force that must be worked with, not against.

It is when a child is like a rushing brook, a creature of restless energy, that we send him to school. There the teacher must try to channel and organize his energy for his own good and for society.

In the classroom fifteen, thirty, or even more children find themselves gathered closely together for an extended time. The problems of living and working together can become intense. And a certain order must prevail so that learning can happen. All this can be very trying for the children. And the teacher must tame these torrents, each one unique and precious, so that each child can make the most of his own talents and the learning opportunities he has before him.

The hickory stick, paddle, and ruler have been the tools for maintaining discipline in the past. Mark Twain gave a vivid description of their use and effects in Tom Sawyer. B. F. Skinner cited some more extreme cases of discipline by whip, cane, and clenched fist. But most teachers, we know, want to be and are in fact humane. While the children's vitality, curiosity, and restless energy do pose management problems in the classroom, teachers prefer not to punish, scowl, shout, or lecture in anger. But how, then, can a teacher maintain reasonable order, teach the children, and be positive?

   Henry David Thoreau tried to be a positive and effective teacher, tried to avoid the physical punishment of the young which was so prevalent in his day. But when a parent pressured him to paddle a child, he did, and then resigned the teaching position he had held for only a few months.

   Mr. Chips found his way from ineffectiveness and punishment in the classroom to humane and significant teaching. But the art of putting together concern, wit, and knowledge can much more easily be admired than imitated. Are there any specific procedures a teacher can follow?

   A certain type of answer to the teacher's need is now beginning to take shape. It incorporates certain aspects of scientific measuring; it acknowledges the complexity of human behavior pointed out by the psychologists; and then it asks, given this particular child, how do we maximize his potential? This system also recognizes the needs of the teacher for reasonable order, it creates an environment for learning, and has the benefits of a positive approach. And that's what this book is about.

   This new system emphasizes the frequent use of positive reinforcements when teaching, the limited use of punishment, the initial analysis of the child, the explicit statement of goals, and the organization of a teaching program that will take the child from where he is to where he can go by sensitive and precise steps.

   There is a growing number of books about the principles of operant conditioning and behavior modification. All that

I know, however, have been written by scholars who tell about their research and the results of their own studies; but they generally have a limited acquaintance with the classroom teacher's perspective, problems, and language. The scholar's work has typically been done with special funding and extra staff. The classroom teacher still stands alone in trying to apply the new discoveries in educational science and technology.

There is today another exciting movement in education, the emergence of teachers with classroom experience who are writing incisively about their difficulties, philosophy, and new methods in the schools. John Holt is probably the most productive of these authors. They advocate a more humane, individualized, and environmentally rich classroom. This thrust from the reality of classroom experience will, I believe, eventually merge with the behavior modification movement. And this book will be a step toward that merger.

This book was written by a teacher who is well acquainted with the classroom, the demands of preparing lessons, marking papers, solving children's problems, and meeting with parents. She knows the tired feet and the sore throat that often accompany a full day of teaching. Sister Helen is a teacher who cares for children as individuals and knows how to make behavior modification work for their benefit.

Sister Helen Shipman began teaching before she was twenty-one, with more than forty children in her classroom. While teaching Indians in Arizona, ghetto children in Chicago, and the poor children in her home community of Sault Ste. Marie, Michigan, she worked for her bachelor's degree and earned a reputation as a competent teacher.

Sister had been teaching for twelve years when I first met her in a summer program using behavior modification. She was scheduled to teach fourth grade in the fall in Sault Ste. Marie. We had part of that class in our summer program.

This particular class had been, for each of the previous teachers, extremely difficult. One child in particular contributed most to the riotous behavior. He rarely sat still for more than a minute; he was oppositional, a clown, and hyperactive. But with the behavior modification program, this child soon worked eagerly, well, and for as long as an hour and a half at one time. The program used instructional materials at the child's level, abundant praise and recognition, and a token system of rewards for good behavior. The tokens were redeemable for treats and fun activities.

Sister decided to continue these procedures for this child during the regular school year and to extend them to the entire class. The system worked amazingly well, and she summarized her experience in a paper titled, "Clugies, Snirkles, and Models--Three Systems of Token Reinforcement in the Grade School Classroom." The paper did not tell about the large number of visitors who came to observe that classroom. One group was examining behavior modification projects throughout the state of Michigan. They saw projects supported by tens of thousands of dollars, and they were most impressed by what Sister Helen had done with encouragement and the limited resources she could secure: an aide from the local school office, some additional instructional materials, and three dollars a year from the parents of each child. With this she performed miracles with problem children including several who had been excluded from the public school.

The following year Sister Helen served as a master teacher for the Head Start program in Sault Ste. Marie, then went into the inner-citylike schools of Highland Park near Detroit. Equipped with goodies and trinkets and a new, systematic approach to behavior management, she found that children could change from almost continuous disruption to steady work if they could earn tokens and then purchase items and activities of their own choice.

Sister Helen's next goal was to extend the behavior modification system from individual students and classrooms to an entire school. She did this at St. Bride's School in Chicago's South Shore, a community then undergoing rapid racial change. This was a real test of her skill in using behavior modification and in training others to use it. Could the procedures be applied from grades one through eight in a coordinated way? Could the teachers carry out the procedures over an entire year? Could the necessary materials and volunteers be found for the program? Would the parents accept the system with its explicit material rewards? The answer was "yes" to all these questions.

This book reflects all these experiences and Sister Helen's study of operant conditioning and behavior modification research. Most of all, it is one teacher talking to others. Teachers want to teach as effectively as they can. Behavior modification can provide significant help.

Behavior modification is not a cure-all for the problems of education, but it is a significant step toward combining a humane concern for children with effective teaching. Sister Helen's involvement and experience testifies to the compatibility of humane concern and scientific methods in teaching children.

James Breiling, Ph.D.
Institute for Behavioral Research
Silver Spring, Maryland

introduction

Jim's file folder was bigger than anyone else's in the school records office. He had been evaluated and tested, counseled and probationed more than anyone else. All of Jim's teachers felt they had failed him. He was loud, belligerent, disruptive, obnoxious, and at times lovable. His behavior ruined classes, but his occasional repentance pulled at his teachers' heartstrings and made them try again, only to fail again.

    Jim was going to be in my class and I dreaded it. I was grasping for straws and I eagerly seized the chance to have Jim's parents enroll him in a summer program for children classified as "highly resistive to change." This program was directed by Dr. Paul Sullivan in Brimley, Michigan. One of the staff psychologists, Dr. James Breiling, worked with Jim and taught him how to read by using contingency contracts and token reinforcers.

    After two weeks in the program, Jim's attention span stretched from ten seconds to ninety minutes and his IQ score jumped almost twenty points!

It sounds incredible. But so do the other examples from my own experience once I had learned to use behavior modification in the classroom. Elizabeth Foley works with me. Some of the examples in this book are from her personal experiences. They are equally true and equally amazing.

The methods we use and recommend are not new. Good teachers everywhere have been using them for generations. Our behavior management system simply combines familiar techniques in a unique way to provide a new kind of learning opportunity for children.

Think back to your own childhood. What teacher do you remember as your favorite? Chances are it was the one who made you feel good about yourself. You may not remember the grade or the subject, but you will remember that you either did well in the class or that the teacher took extra time to help you through the course.

This new approach is getting a lot of attention because the systematic and consistent use of positive reinforcement brings astounding results in a short time. It really works. If I had not been an effective teacher using traditional methods for ten years, I would not have been half so impressed with my first introduction to positive reinforcement. As a convert, however, and as a teacher, I firmly believe that positive reinforcement is the most efficient way to teach and a thoroughly humane way to deal with people. By looking for the good in people and building this up, we give them a good feeling about themselves. At this point, with self-esteem and self-confidence, real learning can begin.

This book is a how-to-do-it manual for teachers. Neither Miss Foley nor I are psychologists or therapists. We are teachers. We know what it is to have forty children in front of us, a beautiful science demonstration going, and the fire alarm ring for a drill. We know about collecting milk money, finding Johnny's lunch, and filling out a three-page questionnaire the principal wants "right now." The examples we give are all from our own experience. All the suggestions have been used successfully. But each teacher and

and each class has a unique personality, and you must decide how you can adapt the suggestions in this book to yourself and to your class.

I have used this behavior management system when I was the only teacher in the school using it. I have used it in a team teaching situation, and I have been part of a program which involved the whole school. It is still rare for a whole school to adopt a token economy system. More often you will be the only one using the tokens. That doesn't matter. When others see what can happen, they will ask for information.

We are grateful to many people for their help and inspiration in preparing this book, especially our parents, our first teachers; Dr. Paul W. Sullivan who introduced us to behavior modification; Dr. and Mrs. James Breiling for much positive reinforcement; our colleagues Sister Lorraine Pepin, Mrs. Joyce Milligan, and Mr. Paul Koonter; Sister Suzanne Doolin and the faculty of St. Bride School, Chicago; Mr. Andrew Brusca and the faculty of Thomson School, Highland Park, Michigan; the Neighborhood Service Organization in Highland Park for encouragement to write; Mrs. Louise Wilkerson who helped develop the SCAN plan; and the people at Loyola University Press for their enthusiasm and assistance.

HJS & EAF

1

Positive Teaching

Any Teacher Can . . . is a book for teachers who want to teach and who don't want to spend most of their time scolding, hollering, and trying to establish order. It is a systematic approach to behavior management based on three simple principles: 1) praise the good; 2) ignore inappropriate behavior as much as possible; and 3) be consistent.

The principles are simple, but they involve a radically different approach to dealing with children. The approach is different, but it is one that any teacher can learn. It doesn't require a Ph.D. in child psychology, just a little common sense, an understanding of the three simple principles above, and a willingness to stick to them until they prove themselves in practice in your classroom.

Speaking about the teacher-student relationship in general, we can say that any type of attention which the teacher gives the student reinforces the behavior for which the attention is given. Accordingly, if you pay attention to disorderly or disruptive conduct, you reinforce that. The student needs attention, and by your conduct you "teach" him that he can get this attention by misbehaving.

On the other hand, if you praise the good and pay attention to appropriate behavior, you will reinforce that and you will be teaching the student that he can get your attention and approval by his good conduct and good study habits. It is as simple as that.

Positive reinforcement means spending the time you're going to spend on behavior management anyway in emphasizing the good rather than correcting the bad. The theory sounds easy, but it takes an effort to "be positive" when your first impulse is to "correct." It actually requires a whole new way of thinking and acting, but it pays off in rich rewards both for your students and for you.

Positive reinforcement can be as simple a thing as a look of approval or a touch on the shoulder. The point is to reinforce the good and ignore the bad. Hence any appropriate recognition, a smile, a gesture, a pat on the back, a word of praise, any of these can serve as positive reinforcement.

One very effective means of positive reinforcement is a system of tokens which we will describe in Chapter Five. The tokens can be anything that can be handed out easily on the spot to reinforce positive behavior. The token system has several advantages for beginners: 1) it focuses the student's attention on something concrete, an immediate reward; 2) because it is negotiable for something of the student's own choice, it eliminates the need to think up an individual reward for the individual student; and 3) having tokens in your hand serves to focus your attention on being positive; they remind you to look for something good to give them for.

But, to repeat, anything will serve for positive reinforcement. Classroom privileges are an excellent incentive; being first in line for recess, being "chosen" to collect class papers, earning the privilege of erasing the board, and so on. Classroom chores like these, almost anything which helps the teacher, can be considered a privilege in a positive reinforcement context. If you learn to see things this way, you will find that students will work doubly hard just to earn the privilege of helping out with such routine duties as monitoring and taking attendance. It all goes back to the notion of recognition. Everybody wants to be somebody special, to be singled out for a little attention and praise.

This is the basic concept behind the whole positive reinforcement principle. It has been scientifically proved, and you know it from your own experience, that praise works wonders. Given enough time and an earnest effort, it will work for you.

Adult Attention Is Very Reinforcing

If you reflect for a moment on your own experience, you will notice that most people ignore the good in others or take it for granted, and they generally pay attention to faults, misconduct, or disturbances. Notice what can happen in the classroom when this procedure is reversed.

Jerry was particularly obnoxious when officials like the principal or superintendent came to visit the class. I was describing Jerry's behavior to Mr. Davis, the superintendent of schools, one day, and he was anxious to see how Jerry reacted to positive reinforcement as opposed to the traditional scolding method of behavior management.

As soon as Mr. Davis arrived at the door of the classroom, Jerry began to talk as loudly as he could. I had prompted Mr. Davis beforehand to ignore any disruptive behavior in the class. So he ignored Jerry's talking, and Jerry began to talk even louder, "Hey, Mr. Davis, look at this pencil." I then began to praise other students for their work, occasionally giving them tokens for their industry. Jerry tried even harder to get attention. He began to rock his desk and oink like a pig. I walked over near Jerry's desk and began to reward the children who were working in spite of the distracting noises. Jerry continued his rocking and oinking. Then I asked one student if he would like to show Mr. Davis our latest science project. I told him that because he had worked so hard, he could show Mr. Davis how the class had collected and mounted insects. Now Jerry loved this sort of privilege, so he picked up his pencil and began to write his name. When he did this, I praised him for beginning his work. As soon as Jerry began working a math problem, I gave him additional tokens. I reinforced Jerry rather heavily as often as I could for continuing his work. Mr. Davis then walked by Jerry's desk, patted him on the head, and said, "Keep up the good work, Jerry." The boy never even raised his eyes but kept right on working. I could see he had a smile on his face.

Just as Mr. Davis was about to leave the room, Jerry raised his hand and the superintendent acknowledged him. Jerry asked if he would like to see the geography maps, because his work was now complete. The superintendent glanced at me for a clue. And I said, "Certainly, Jerry, because you have completed your work, you may show Mr. Davis the maps."

Adult attention is very reinforcing, either for good or bad behavior. In the case I just described, Jerry learned that I would not pay attention to him for his loud talking, his oinking or rocking. He then tried to get the attention he wanted from the students around him. But when he saw they were getting rewards and tokens for working hard and ignoring him, Jerry learned that he would only get attention for good behavior.

A Student Must Feel Good About Himself Before He Can Begin To Learn

One of the best things a teacher can do for his students is to look for the good qualities in each one and make as many positive remarks as possible. This is especially important for students who find school difficult or who happen to be slower learners than the rest of the class. We have to treat students as unique human beings. Each one can do something another cannot do, and that "something" is the

8

stepping stone you can use to build his confidence and teach him more difficult tasks and lessons.

Mary was a very chubby fourth grader. She was too large for the regular classroom desks, so a larger one was installed just for her. She was hyperconscious of her size and she was very lazy. Mary was taking medication for her obesity and that partly accounted for her lethargy. But whatever the cause, Mary seemed to lack incentive for anything. She didn't especially care about earning tokens either. She had only one real ambition in life and that was to be a ballerina. Mary read books about the petite dancers who pirouette with handsome young royalty. This was the key.

I made arrangements for an eighth grade ballet student to give Mary lessons once a week if she would complete all her class assignments. In the first month of ballet lessons Mary lost five pounds. Her parents were so delighted with what was happening that they soon offered the eighth grade ballet teacher a stipend for her help. Mary's self-image rose 100 percent. She felt good about herself. The best part came when the principal asked Mary to dance in the school musical production. Mary's grades rose from C's and D's to A's and B's in three marking periods.

Jimmy was a second grader who spent two years in first grade with little more accomplished than that he could recognize the letters of the alphabet and the numbers from one to ten. Yet Jimmy had an amazing facility with tools. I discovered this quite by accident one day when he came to class with a screwdriver in his pocket. He explained that the pencil sharpener was not fastened securely and that a simple adjustment of the fasteners would eliminate the problem of the point always breaking off the sharpened pencil. And he was right. Jimmy fixed the pencil sharpener and this major improvement made everybody happy. Jimmy got all sorts of attention for his skill and thoughtfulness. The principal happened to be in the hall just then, and I told her about Jimmy's skill with tools. She turned to Jim and said, "When you learn your reading words today, Jim, come up to my office and I'll give you a job to do with your tools." Jimmy was elated and he was never more eager to learn words. He even asked to skip recess so that he could study longer. The word soon got around that Jim could tighten screws and secure mop handles and the first thing we knew he was able to recognize and read every word in his spelling book.

These are examples of positive reinforcement; but they are just that, examples. We could multiply them a hundred times from our experience. But the thing to keep in mind and apply in your own classroom is the common sense notion that every human being seeks recognition. Your recognition of his skills and qualities makes the student feel good about himself and gives him the confidence that he can learn. Love is the greatest reinforcer.

Praise the Good

Did you ever hear students say, "I hate math," or "I hate English"? This kind of remark is often followed by something like this: "That old lady never gives you anything but work. No matter how hard you try, just no way to please her." This kind of statement points to the fact that when a teacher is critical about the student, he usually becomes hostile toward her. Students look upon their work as part of themselves. When they receive critical remarks about their work, they take it as criticism of themselves, and they react accordingly.

In view of the basic principle we mentioned above about everyone wanting recognition, you can see that criticism is counter-productive. It expends time and energy in the wrong direction. The teacher who criticizes pays attention to and reinforces the wrong behavior. So the emphasis of all your teaching must be positive.

I once participated in a pilot program to teach creative

writing through personal experiences. All the language arts skills were built into the program, along with the effort to develop the fantasy life and creative abilities of the intermediate level student.

I began by telling the class about my silly fear of heights. I built up the introduction until the students were bursting with enthusiasm to tell their own stories about their own silly fears. I then asked them to write them down. No points would be taken off for misspelling or poor grammar. The whole idea was to make the silly fear become real for someone else.

Each student did a fantastic job of creating a silly fear composition. I read each paper and made an appropriate comment on it. The comments were all positive and complimentary, citing creativity and vivid narration. No other comments were made.

On the following day when I returned the papers to the students, they felt good about the papers and about themselves. Each paper had some positive comment. This was such a different experience from former English classes where the student would get his paper back all red with corrections and the inevitable C or D on the bottom. And he would promptly discard it.

This time the students were proud to show their compositions to other members of the class, and I had some read the best ones aloud for everyone.

Later on in the lesson I wrote ten misspelled words and ten improperly punctuated phrases on the board. These words and phrases worked like magic. As the words and phrases appeared, the brighter students recognized the errors and those who had made the errors discovered their own mistakes. The discoveries were very subtle. No one was singled out as guilty of using a misplaced modifier. Instead, each student was given an opportunity to edit his own composition or to ask the teacher or another student for specific help. The enthusiasm was high and the individual attitude toward English composition was vastly improved.

When you look for the good in people, they are much more likely to listen to you. A very wise mentor once said, "Your students will probably never remember all the major capitols of the world, but Johnny will remember that on February 25th you smiled and complimented him on his new shoes, his neat desk, or on his great contribution to the basketball game.

Teachers who make the most lasting impressions are those who care more about people than about bushels of wheat per acre or correct answers on a test. It is not that these things are unimportant, but they have to be kept in their proper perspective.

We all remember teachers who confidently expected that we would perform well, and we did. They never nagged. They expected great things. Nagging is one of the worst faults a teacher can have. It makes the student dependent, unable to think for himself, unable to act on his own initiative. It is also counterproductive from the positive reinforcement standpoint because it pays attention to and hence reinforces the wrong behavior.

Ignore Inappropriate Behavior

This second principle of classroom behavior management may sound easier in theory than it is in practice, but any teacher can do it. Any behavior which is not positive and productive should be ignored as much as possible. It takes effort and persistence, and it is hard to get used to at first. The idea of "letting some kid get away with something" dies hard. And every teacher is at least initially terrified by the thought that by ignoring misbehavior he or she may be opening the door to chaos.

Some children will deliberately act up just to get your attention or test your reaction. This should be ignored. No eye contact; even this is a way of giving attention. Rather walk over to the students who are busy and reinforce them for working hard. Then, out of the corner of your eye, watch for some good behavior by the culprit and reinforce him for that. Praise the positive, ignore the negative as much as possible.

Leonard was a walker. The minute I would say, "My, this class is working hard," Leonard would get up and walk around the room or whistle or do something else. Formerly, I would call his name and ask him why he was walking or whistling. With the token system, I would recognize and maybe reward with a token one or other student who was busy, and I would ignore Leonard until he sat down to work.

It is not easy to ignore Leonard when he's walking around, and doing so calls for a mental "shift of gears" by you. But research has proved that when Leonard is ignored he gets to work faster than when he gets attention for deviant behavior.

To some extent it takes faith to begin a system of positive behavior management, and we can't blame anyone for keeping his fingers crossed. In this respect "ignoring inappropriate behavior" is the biggest psychological stumbling block. But the stumbling block is largely mental, based on old concepts of classroom discipline.

In Chapter Seven we'll treat at some length the question of discipline problems and what to do if things seem to be getting out of hand; but for now, make an initial act of faith and try to implement these two principles which are like two sides of the same coin--praise the good, ignore the bad. Students are looking for recognition. When you recognize the good, you will be reinforcing the positive behavior that you want in class. When you ignore the inappropriate, you do not reinforce it and you will be working to eliminate it.

You've Got To Be Consistent

Consistency is the third principle we mentioned at the beginning of this chapter. It is absolutely essential for you, your class, and for any effective teaching.

We often hear teachers say, "I just get my class where

I want them, and it's the end of the year, and I have to start all over again." It really should not take all year to establish a working relationship with your class. It can occur much more quickly, in a few weeks, or even a few days if your methods are consistent. In fact on the first day of school before any teaching can begin, the students have to find out if you are consistent. Predictability of a teacher's behavior is essential for the students. As soon as they know for sure how you are going to react in certain similar situations, they can stop testing and turn their attention to learning. Young people need this security. They have to know where you are and in general what you are going to do.

Students play games to see if the teacher will really do what he says he'll do. You need only evesdrop a little to learn a lot about consistent teachers. This conversation recently came to my attention.

Joe   "Hey Bill, give me your math homework; I didn't do mine."
Bill   "Okay, but she won't collect it anyway."
Sam   "She might collect it, but she won't grade it."
Al   "Yeh, you never know what she wants. Who cares about her anyway. Besides I hate math."
Bill   "You'd be better off doing your English. Mr. Hill always checks the homework."
Joe   "I know. I already did the assignment. English is my favorite subject."

In this brief exchange you can tell that the English teacher is consistent and predictable and the students don't mind working with him because they feel they are learning. The math teacher, however, does not command the same respect. The students don't know what she's going to do, and this makes them feel uneasy and dissatisfied. They do not feel secure because they cannot predict her behavior. Consistency is the key.

But consistency is not just for class assignments, it has to be the keynote of your whole approach to the students. For instance, if you reward positive behavior for awhile and then revert to calling attention to inappropriate behavior, you will lose whatever progress you have made and you will confuse the students. Sure, some students will test your patience at first because they will be testing you. But you've got to resolve to be consistent and pay attention only to positive good behavior.

You've got to be consistent, too, in your rewards. This is particularly critical in the beginning. If you reward an action by one student, you will want to reward similar actions by other students. You'll be tempted to think this is excessive at first, but it will set a positive tone in your class and make the students secure in the knowledge that you are consistent.

Remember that these rewards, either words, gestures, or tokens, are the attention the child is seeking, the recognition he wants and deserves for good behavior. If you reward an action once, you have reinforced it, and the student will do it again to gain the same word of praise or another token. That's when you've got to be consistent too. Consistency is not only the name of the game in behavior management, it makes the whole difference between success and failure in teaching.

Take Jacquie, for instance. Jacquie forgot everything. She'd leave her house in the morning and forget her lunch. When she got home in the afternoon, she would have left her homework books at school. As a result, her mother nagged her and reminded her, her teacher prompted her and nagged her, and Jacquie got worse and worse. Her mother and teacher, of course, were reinforcing Jacquie's forgetfulness by their nagging.

But when Miss Meyer, Jacquie's teacher, first learned about positive reinforcement, things began to change. Miss Meyer gave Jacq lots of encouragement and praise whenever she remembered anything. The positve remarks helped Jacquie. She was being noticed and praised for something good, for remembering. It was a heady feeling for Jacquie. She liked it and she began to remember to bring her books home and her lunch to school. She felt good about herself, and very good about Miss Meyer.

But before Jacquie really got things under control, the class had planned a field trip. The token system was in its initial stages, and Miss Meyer was using the trip as a double incentive for her class. The trip was to be paid for by tokens which the children earned for doing their class work. The trip was also a special incentive for students who did not remember things. Miss Meyer told the class that each student would have to present his ticket in order to get on the bus. Anyone who lost his ticket or failed to bring it would not go to the museum. You guessed it! Jacquie forgot her ticket. She could not go to the museum. Oh! there were tears. And Miss Meyer felt like Miss Meany of 1899; but she was firm and consistent. And Jacquie did not go to the museum.

Was Miss Meyer unfair? Unjust? Mean? If Miss Meyer had given in, Jacquie would have stopped crying, and Miss Meyer would have felt a little better. But in effect it would have been like saying to Jacquie, "That's all right, dear, I really do not mean what I say. You don't have to pay attention to anything I say. I frequently change my mind." But since Miss Meyer was consistent, Jacquie knew that she would have to try harder to remember next time. Jacq learned that "forgetting" had bad consequences, and from that day she began to remember.

In the following chapters we'll take up other aspects of behavior management. We'll go beyond the notion of working for immediate rewards--a smile, a word, a token--to delayed rewards and contingency contracting: "After you've done this assignment, you can have free time to do something else." We'll see how alternate class assignments can be used to motivate slow learners, and how the student's own achievements and learning can become its own reward. That's when you have really succeeded.

But always remember the underlying concept that makes the system work. Children, like all of us, are human beings. They want to succeed. They want to be recognized. They need to be loved. And you can respond to this basic human need and at the same time create a positive classroom atmosphere by paying attention to their good work and good behavior. It's just a matter of following these three simple principles: 1) praise the good; 2) ignore inappropriate behavior; and 3) be consistent.

2

Grandma's Law

I once overheard a junior high student say, "I hate Mondays. That's the day we always have to read a chapter and answer the questions!" Her companion answered with equal disgust, "It isn't Mondays I hate, it's Fridays. We always have a test on Friday." Though their teachers were consistent enough and both students were secure in their anticipation of what was coming, it is surely distasteful to invariably read chapters, write answers, and study for tests. Notice the difference between this approach and that of the teacher who challenges her students with a free period to do "anything within reason" when they have learned all of their material with at least 85 percent accuracy. Silent study with a built-in incentive like this will be highly motivating. Paradoxically, students will work very hard to get out of work. The next time you begin a new chapter and are tempted to say, "Read the chapter and answer . . ." Stop and say, "After you have read the first ten pages of the chapter, and you feel that you know the material, come and let me quiz you on it. If you answer all of my questions satisfactorily, you can help me quiz the other students."

The principle here is to couple a privilege or a more interesting activity to the completion of a specific learning task. It's called contingency contracting, and it's the same simple principle at work in Grandma's Law: When you finish your spinach, you can eat your desert.

Contingency contracting is a further application of the positive reinforcement we discussed in Chapter One. When students do their assignments well, they are rewarded with certain enjoyable events or the opportunity to engage in some preferred activity of their own choice.

We experience contingency contracting in all aspects of life and business and human relations. "If you will work three hours, I will pay you six dollars." "If you take out the garbage, you can go to the movies." "If you cut the lawn, you can use the family car tonight." "If you work fifty weeks, you can have two weeks vacation," and so on. These are all positive contingency contracts in which a definite reward is promised for the accomplishment of a certain specified task. It is based on the principle that people are motivated to do certain tasks by the hope of a desirable reward.

And good teachers have always used this kind of motivation in their teaching, but usually not systematically and often not consistently.

It is peculiar, however, that many teachers use negative contingencies to motivate their students. "If you don't do your homework, you won't pass the test." "If you don't study now, you will fail the course." "If you don't sit down and be quiet, I'll send you to the principal." "If you don't pass this course, you won't get into high school." All of this is directly opposed to the positive approach we are recommending in this behavior management program.

With positive contingency contracting, the teacher makes an agreement with the student under which he promises rewards in return for the desired learning activity by the student. The motivation is just as or more effective than the negative fear, and the whole atmosphere of the class becomes positive and happy rather than negative and threatening. Notice how contingency contracting worked in the following cases.

The students in an eight-week summer school program were scheduled to be in the fourth and fifth grades the following fall, but their reading and math skills were at the primary level. Miss Sullivan, their teacher, spent the first five weeks of the summer school having the students copy three and four number addition columns from the chalkboard, making drawings from "Snow White," and watching cartoon movies. They spent one whole day discussing how they would prepare a picnic for the following day.

These "fun" things could have been made contingent upon productive school work and appropriate behavior. As it was, they were merely used to provide busy work for the students while Miss Sullivan studied for her college courses.

All of the students had been tested in reading and math on the first day of school. After five weeks they had made no significant progress.

In the last three weeks of summer school all extra curricular trips were made contingent upon attendance and productive school work, a token-reward system was introduced, and each child received at least ten minutes of private tutoring every day. After three weeks of contingency contracting and remedial work in basic number combinations, the class's median math score rose 16 percent. It could have been much higher if the contingency contracting and behavior management techniques had been employed earlier in the summer.

These students knew exactly what was expected of them, and they achieved their learning objectives because they had to learn their lessons before they were allowed the privileges or prizes of their choice.

It is significant here that one boy who was the troublemaker of the year with the non-contingent teaching became a model of good behavior when the token system was introduced. Here's what happened.

When summer school began Paul was belligerent. He sat on top of his desk and shouted at the teacher on the first day of school. Paul was always looking for a way to needle anyone who tried to teach him anything. He was gross. He was the kind of boy no teacher wants in class. But when the token system was introduced and Paul realized how many tokens he could earn simply by doing a little school work, he began to work very hard. Since he was more capable than most of the other students, he became a hero by earning more tokens than anyone else. Instead of being the class villain, he became a model of behavior.

Does it sound preposterous? Would you believe that the obnoxious kid that nobody wanted suddenly became a cooperative, industrious student? The story is in fact true.

The formula for contingency contracting is simply this: If you do X (a learning task), then you may do Y (a reinforcing event).

The first step, then, for you the teacher will be to specify the learning tasks for each student, and then to link these tasks with appropriate reinforcers. "If you do these five math problems correctly, you can work on your art project for the rest of the period."

It is critical to the success of this kind of programming to know what the student likes to do and what he is really interested in. In order to be worthwhile and effective the rewards must be really desirable and not otherwise available to the student.

As for desirability, you will find that the student himself is generally the best source of information on what is reinforcing to him at any given time. Notice how Miss White discovered what Donald really wanted and then used this information to motivate his learning.

Donald liked to be alone, and he regularly withdrew from the activities of the other students. He was not interested in tokens either. They had little meaning for him except that he felt badly when he didn't have any to use at the "store." When this happened Donald would flare into a rage and become almost uncontrollable. He came from a large family, a disorganized home. One day Miss White, his teacher, noticed that Donald worked quite well in an isolated area or on a one-to-one basis with the teacher. So she used this little bit of information to create a quiet area where Donald could work alone. She moved a file cabinet into the corner of the room and put Donald's desk behind it. This was Donald's office; it was not a punishment area, but a privileged area, and Donald had to pay rent in tokens for the space. He earned the tokens by working on his class assignments.

Donald was very proud of his office and made signs to tape on the cabinet which indicated whether he was in or out. When Donald was in, the sign read "Open." When he was at a special class, the office was "Closed."

This little arrangement, simple as it was, was just what Donald needed to be a "special" person, not one of the crowd. This special attention changed Donald from being a troublemaker and a truant to a boy with 100 percent attendance and 100 percent completion of his work. By doing his assignments, Donald earned tokens to pay the "rent" for his office. He now had a motive for studying and his work began to improve.

A very tall gentleman once told me that he had always wanted to sit in the front seat when he was a boy in school, but because of his height he usually sat in the back of the class. It would have been easy for his teachers to capitalize on his wish to sit up front. These are the kinds of things, if teachers are sensitive to them, that can make a contingency contracting system very effective.

Here again, Grandma's Law applies: First clean up your plate, and then you can have your desert.

The critical factor in contingency contracting is for the

teacher to find out what the student likes to do so that she can link this with the learning task at hand. You can do this simply by observing what the students choose to do when given the freedom and the opportunity. This activity can then be used as an effective reinforcer in a contingency contract.

My four-year-old nephew loves to have someone read him a story. Whenever we want him to do a certain task, we say, "As soon as you do this or this, then we can read a story." He will then complete such difficult and distasteful tasks as putting on his pajamas for bed, taking a nap in the afternoon, picking up toys, or cleaning his plate. The contingency tactic never fails.

In school it is easy to say, "As soon as you finish your reading lesson, you may work on your science project." Or, "When you learn your ten spelling words for today, you may have free time until two o'clock." Always be clear and specific about what is required and what the reward will be. The task requirements should always be within the student's ability to accomplish. Small approximations should be contracted and rewarded rather than large, long-range tasks. "When you master the equations, you can listen to the tape recorder" would be a poor contract. The task is too large and too unspecified.

Remember, too, that the more immediately a reward follows upon the accomplishment of the task, the more effective it will be.

If you happen to get into a situation in which you must teach required material which you feel your students have already mastered, you might have them write their own contingency contracts to fulfill the requirement, and then on the completion of it, have the assurance of being able to do a preferred activity.

Miss Dwyer, an eighth grade teacher, felt that the required spelling exercises were less sophisticated than her group's needs. She divided each spelling unit into ten lessons

24

and told her class that a forty-minute period was provided for spelling. During that period they were free to do any school activity they wished as soon as they passed each spelling lesson with 90 percent accuracy. Tokens were given as an added incentive for accurate completion of the written portions of the workbook. A large bonus of tokens was also given to the student when he finished each unit of ten lessons. All the spelling books were completed well before the deadlines and accuracy checks proved that the free time was a highly successful reinforcement.

Notice how Miss Dwyer specified the tasks and immediately rewarded the successful accomplishment of each segment of the spelling lessons.

At the beginning you will want to arrange contingencies with individual students, but the aim of a good contingency contracting system is to lead the student from teacher-controlled contingencies to self-controlled planning. It leads to a healthy independence and self-determination. But this will come with time and experience.

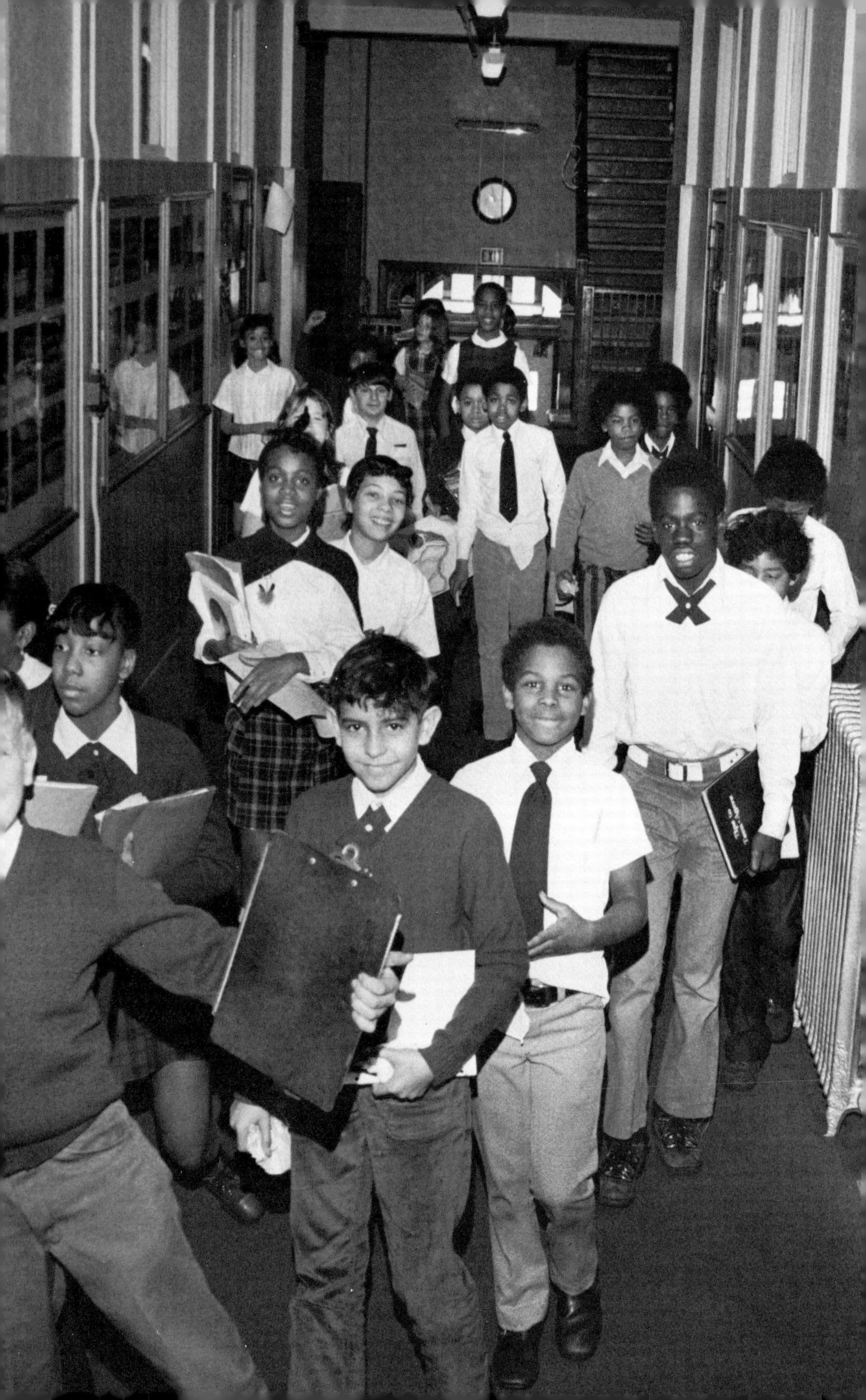
EXIT

3

How To Begin

With the general principles of positive reinforcement and contingency contracting set out, we now come to the more immediate preparation for effective teaching, getting to know your students and identifying appropriate materials for their instruction.

Getting To Know Your Students

The first task you have here will be to find out just where each student is academically, what his strengths and weaknesses are, what his likes and dislikes are. You can use diagnostic tests for this purpose, IQ scores, or achievement tests. But no one test should predetermine a child's abilities in your mind. The scores will be helpful indicators, but the wise teacher will only use them along with her own intuitive understanding of each child.

The teacher who uses a contingency contracting program has to know the students even better. What are their interests, hobbies, leisure activities? What are their favorite sports, their favorite music, their favorite anything? You can discover these things by careful listening, by socializing with the class, by observing what they choose to do in their free time. The students might even be asked to make a list of their favorite things.

For planning and management purposes, it will be very helpful to have a record for each child in your class listing the learning and skills objectives of the course, with indications of which objectives the student has mastered and which he has yet to learn. The more information you have about your students, the easier it will be to give appropriate assignments and appropriate reinforcements to each one.

Mr. Melbourn knew very little about his students. The noise from his class came right through the brick wall. It wasn't until the first marking period, however, that the principal decided Mr. Melbourn should seek employment elsewhere. He made a fatal mistake. Mr. Melbourn made out his quarter grades on the class list which was issued the first day of school. Two of the students on the list had moved over the summer and had never shown up for classes in the fall. Yet Mr. Melbourn gave each of them a "C" for math and a comment about their poor study habits. Mr. Melbourn had not really gotten to know his students.

A teacher needs to know his pupils not only to grade them, but to help them choose appropriate life models and ways of doing things that are suitable to their own personalities. A teacher is a tremendous role model, probably the most important person to influence a youngster after his parents.

Preparing Materials

Once you have a fairly good idea of where your students are, you will want to be sure you have suitable learning materials for them; that is, materials that are interesting and relevant.

Appropriate materials are essential for effective teaching and learning. When students have a good curriculum with materials and learning opportunities well suited to "where they are," behavior problems are much less likely to occur.

Examine your textbooks to be sure the vocabulary and interest level is suited to your students. It can be very harmful to give a student a book that is too difficult for him. And he may very well be insulted if you give him one that is below his reading level. It will be best to have a variety of materials at hand that run for several grades below your grade level to several grades above.

What we are proposing here, and what we were assuming in the first two chapters of the book, is some type of individualized instruction. The teacher who tries to heap the same assignment on a widely diverse group of children is asking for trouble. This kind of assignment is bound to be too difficult for the slow learner and too easy, therefore boring, for the quicker student. Lesson assignments have to be divided up, programmed, and adapted to the individual needs of the individual student.

To prepare your materials for contingency contracting and positive reinforcement, you will first want to specify the educational objectives of your subject area, no matter what it is. Then break the subject matter down into small task segments. Next line up the instructional materials, alternate exercises, and research projects that will help the student acquire the skill or information you have specified in each task segment. These materials, exercises, and projects should, ideally, be short enough to be completed and rewarded in one class period. It will be good for you to write each of these small learning tasks on a card so that they can easily be contracted. With this kind of programming, contingency contracting, and positive reinforcement, your students will be able to move step-by-step from where they are to the skills and knowledge goals set out in the course objectives.

Students who show greater capacities can be directed toward the research projects. By using a token system for positive reinforcement, you can "pay" students for outside research. At the beginning they will be excited by the possibility of earning tokens, but as they get more and more involved in discovering new information, learning will become its own reward and the tokens can gradually be withdrawn. This is a delicate process, but the sensitive teacher will be able to tell when the tokens are helpful and when the students can move ahead on their own interior motivation.

It is easy to motivate the capable student. It is also easy to motivate the slower learner if you give him a goal within his reach, one that he can achieve without too much difficulty. He does not want to feel inferior, and he will just as readily do research as the other members of the class.

In an intermediate class, for instance, you can design research projects on different levels. The more capable science student may be given the option of building a box camera, an electric circuit, or a model space ship. A slower learner may collect leaves and match them with samples already mounted. Children can get very involved in the study of prehistoric animals. They will also be fascinated by the study of plant circulation which can be seen by placing a stalk of celery in a glass of colored water.

Brighter students can move vertically when programmed material is being used, but a slower learner must have a variety of similar or lateral exercises so that he can repeat the experience and gain the security of learning a particular lesson well enough to go on to the next one. He needs the assurance from the teacher that he is constantly improving and doing so very successfully. This is where positive reinforcement in the form of recognition, praise, encouragement, or tokens is so important and so valuable. The slow learner may also need a greater variety of "fun" exercises. You can give students tokens for their good work and allow them to spend them in listening corners, reading areas, or working on special projects.

Students insist on interesting subject matter. All across the country for the past few years we have heard complaints about how irrelevant much of the school curriculum is, how bored the students are. How relevant is a foreign language for students who scarcely speak English? What about white ethnic schools in the midst of a predominantly black or Chicano population? How relevant is the complex basic math system for inner-city kids when the local store sells canned corn for thirteen cents and then advertises the same item on sale, two cans for twenty-eight cents? Students want to learn something they can use. Math has meaning for them when it is used to measure a floor or carpet, or cake mix for a cake, or when it is used to calculate the flight of a homemade missile. But it means little as an abstract science. The student wants to roll up his sleeves and participate. He gets bored as a bystander.

If you are faced with inadequate teaching materials, then you must improvise according to the needs of your students. Few school systems are faced with extreme poverty of materials, but one public school summer program I knew had nothing more to offer than one pencil for every two students and one piece of paper per student per week. A very ingenious teacher was able to establish a fine remedial program by using newspapers, magazines, cereal boxes and other such printed material.

In systems where finances are not a problem, curriculum consultants are invaluable. One special teacher was on the verge of resigning because he could not obtain the text materials required for his class. He did not know how to contact the curriculum consultant. In fact, he didn't even know there was such a person on the staff. It is always good to investigate your school system to discover all its available resources.

In summary, then, your immediate preparation as you begin the school year will be to get to know your students and then to divide appropriate learning materials into small task segments so they can be contracted efficiently and the students can easily move from one learning achievement to the next. You will then be ready to start.

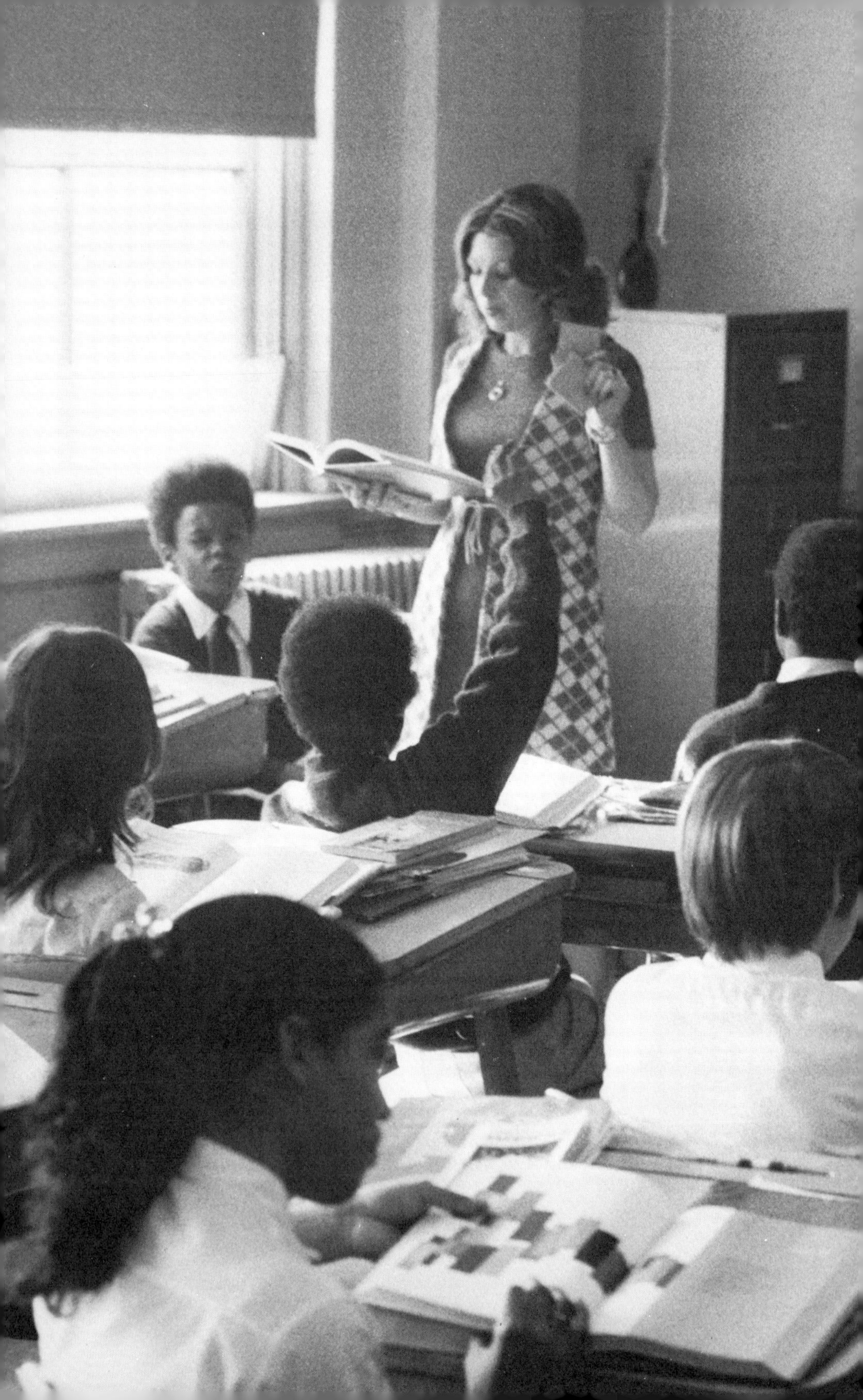

4
Ground Rules

Thus far we have considered the three principles of positive teaching, the practice of contingency contracting, and, briefly, how to prepare materials for systematic, individualized instruction. But what to do on Monday morning at nine o'clock?

There is no need to wait until you have a behavior problem to establish some Ground Rules for conduct in class. It is good to do so on the first day of school and set the tone right away for the entire year.

You can start by having a class discussion about what constitutes acceptable behavior. The main emphasis should be on respect for others, and the class discussion should involve as many of the students as possible. "What sort of Ground Rules do we need so that everyone can live and work and learn together?" It will be good to have someone write all the proposals on the chalkboard.

You should acknowledge and encourage each suggestion with comments like, "Very good, Oscar." "That's an excellent point, Beth." "I never thought of that, LeRoy," or similar remarks.

When the class has proposed all the Ground Rules they think will be necessary, ask them to look over the suggestions on the board and see which ones are similar. For example, someone may have said, "Don't talk while someone else is talking." And another suggestion might have been, "Pay attention when the teacher is teaching." Point out to the students that these are similar statements and could be made into one. Continue to compare the suggestions and you will find that most of them will boil down to two or three important points. We have usually gotten down to a few succinct Ground Rules like these: 1) Raise your hand to speak or ask questions; 2) Stay in your seat; 3) Do your work.

Remember to keep the rules clear and simple. "Do your work" is a good rule because the students can easily understand and obey it, and you can easily reward them for doing so. "Stay in your seat" and "Raise your hand . . ." are also good, clear rules. It is easy to reinforce students for obeying them.

Another guide for forming rules is that they should be positive. An example of a negative rule is "Do not talk." Negative rules tend to arouse hostilities in children, and they are not in keeping with the positive aspects of our behavior management program.

When the rules are vague or ambiguous, it is like having no rules at all. For example, rules like "Be kind" or "Do your best" are too vague. To some children "Be kind" means to share candy with a friend at recess. "Do your best" might mean be neat, or it might mean almost anything. Another problem with vague rules is that they do not require behavior that is observable. For a rule to be good in a behavioral sense, it has to require something that can easily be observed and rewarded.

Ground Rules should be short, clear, and they must be posted in the classroom in a conspicuous place. It would be a mistake to assume that the class knows the rules and they need not be posted. Having the rules clearly visible is a valuable silent reminder. Get a piece of cardboard and print them in large letters.

Check from time to time to see if your rules are really necessary for good behavior in class. The rule "Stay in your seat" is a good starting rule to prevent "walkers" from too much aimless travel, but this rule may be discarded as soon as purposeful activity away from the seat is permissible.

You will probably want to revise your Ground Rules from time to time, especially if you are working from whole class instruction toward individualized instruction with contracts. It has to be clear to students whether quiet talking and walking around will be permitted. Life is full of motion and movement is a sign of healthy growth. Only that noise which keeps others from learning really has to be quieted. But students do need to be taught respect for one another. You can do this by positively reinforcing considerateness and thoughtfulness of others.

I recently visited a classroom where positive reinforcement was being used with individualized instruction. It was intriguing. Everyone was doing something different. One group of students was over in a corner watching a movie. A girl was reading at her desk while petting a furry animal. A boy was lying on the floor doing math problems on a large sheet of wrapping paper. The teacher was in another corner working with a small group on a science project. There was a quiet hum of activity in the room, but it was purposeful activity. Students were looking at charts, examining displays, signing sheets. Every child seemed to be about his business without being a distraction to anyone else.

These fourth graders were so self-disciplined and so interested in their school work that they paid no attention to the visitors who entered the room. This was a free classroom and one where learning was certainly taking place. In fact, learning had become its own reward. This did not happen overnight. The teacher had used tokens to train the students to be responsible and to keep working. They knew what the teacher wanted, class rules were posted in a conspicuous place, and the teacher regularly praised and rewarded good behavior.

Back to Monday morning. Once you have set up clear, concise Ground Rules, your next step will be to begin reinforcing the students for obeying them. People continue to do the things for which they are rewarded, and they generally stop doing those things for which they receive no reward. So you will want to develop an attitude of watching for every positive performance you can see and praising the students for them. Couple your verbal praise with a token as often as you can.

When Christopher raises his hand to ask a question, you might walk over to his desk, give him a token, and say, "Thanks, Chris, for raising your hand. How can I help you?" This way, Chris learns that good behavior pays off. He gets attention from you, and he contributes to a good learning environment in the class.

Vary the kinds of reinforcement you use. Verbal praise, tokens, or tactile praise can all be used together or interchangeably as the situation suggests. There are many ways to recognize and praise a student. Different expressions should be used in different circumstances.

Children of all ages appreciate tactile as well as verbal praise. Little children especially relish a hug. Other students appreciate a pat on the back as a sign of approval. Others like a handshake of victory.

You can also make the entire class feel good by saying "You have all been so good this morning, I'm going to give you five minutes extra at recess."

After recess be very positive about whatever good behavior you saw on the playground or on the way back to the classroom. Try to ignore the inappropriate.

Once again, praise and reinforce the first child who answered the bell and came into school without a special invitation. "Tina, you may pass out these papers because you were the first to answer the bell." When you add, "I am very proud of you, Tina," you will make others try to remember to come promptly the next day. They will all want the extra bit of recognition, so be sure to watch carefully for the prompt response and give praise accordingly.

It is important to give praise and tokens frequently for all different kinds of good behavior. Reinforce the students often, but not for the same thing. Handing out tokens must not become automatic or a form of bribery. If a student asks for a token, it should not be given.

Remember to identify all the rewards you give. "Valerie, you may take this note to the office because you were the first to begin your work after recess." In this instance a token is optional since the reward is immediate and social in nature. The child is recognized for his good behavior. He is being rewarded immediately with a privilege.

At the beginning this reinforcement system requires a lot of time and effort and a special awareness on your part. It demands an alertness to each individual student. So much praising and passing out of tokens may seem a waste of time and effort, but it will prove to be a small enough price when compared with the academic advances children can make when they develop study habits usually attributed to much older students.

In my former teaching experience I always felt good if the class managed to fairly well complete each of their textbooks in the course of the year. But the first year I used positive reinforcement, the children worked so hard and so efficiently that we covered four reading books and four workbooks that year as well as completing the English, science, social studies, and math courses.

The big difference, as far as I could tell, was that formerly I was spending at least half of my time scolding, correcting, admonishing, and restoring order, whereas now I used this time for instruction and helping the students learn.

With the token system, you can walk around and acknowledge good behavior without even stopping your instruction. The tokens do the work.

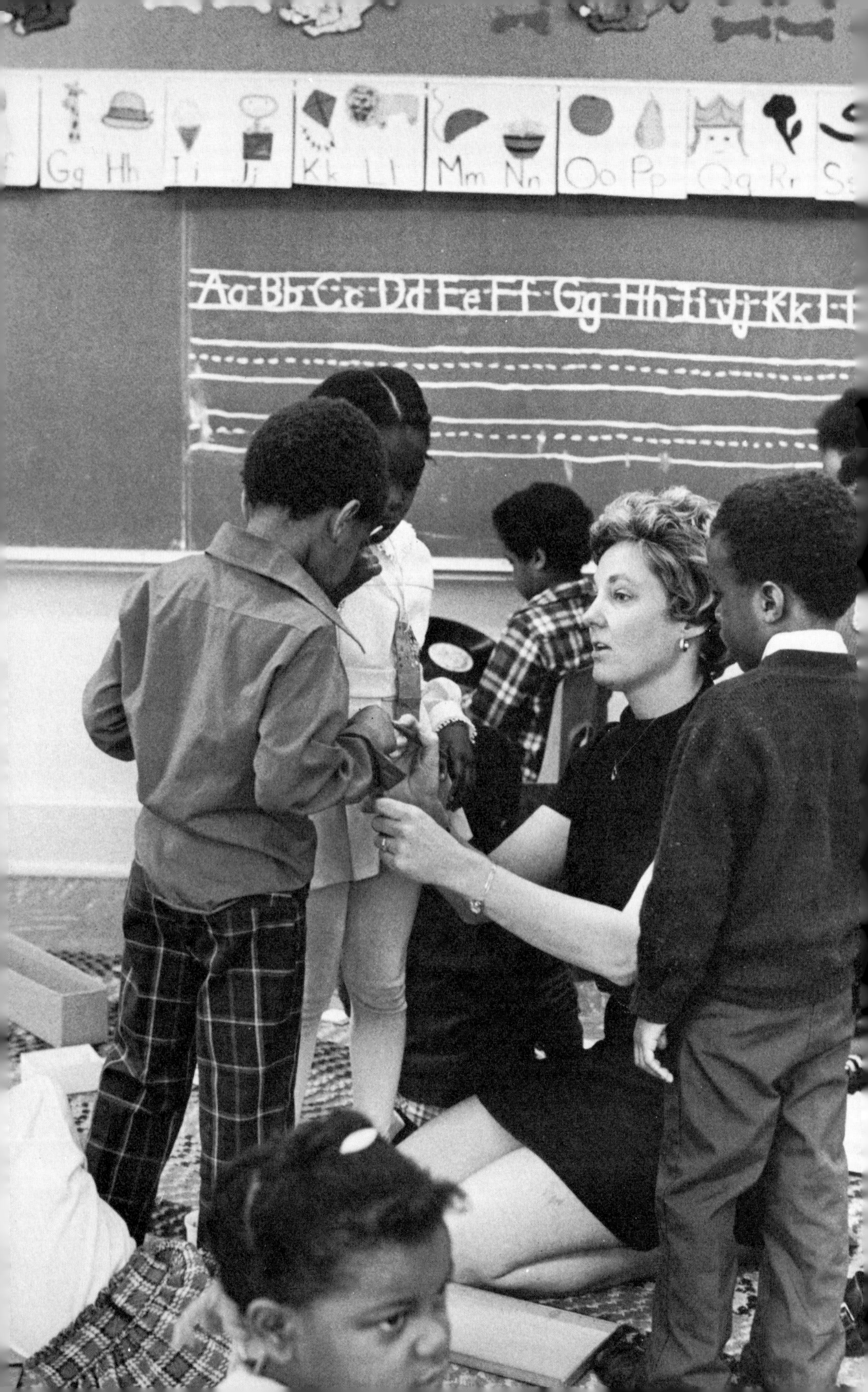
Gg Hh Ii Jj Kk Ll Mm Nn Oo Pp Qq Rr Ss
Aa Bb Cc Dd Ee Ff Gg Hh Ii Jj Kk

5

A Token Economy

Up to now we have assumed the use of some form of token system, but we have not said much about the token itself. The only rule to follow is that the token should be such that it cannot be easily duplicated. The tokens are valuable, the temptation is great, and student ingenuity is often amazing.

Some types of tokens we have seen include pieces of tagboard, mimeographed paper, metal washers, poker chips, plastic counters, and used IBM cards. Some work better than others. Used IBM cards cut into thirds or quarters are both inexpensive and easily obtained from companies with computers. These should be stamped, however, with the rubber stamp of the school because would-be-counterfeiters can get cards just as easily as you can.

If you teach small children, the tokens should be soft, silent, and made of some material that can weather moist little hands, nervous teeth, and a trip through the wash and rinse cycles of the family Maytag.

Some children are too young to manage tokens at all. One kindergarten teacher in Chicago hung a large paper disk on a fairly long string around the neck of each child. She gave positive reinforcement by punching a hole in the disk every time the child completed a task or did something very good.

When I first began a positive reinforcement system, I used graph paper for each child. This was taped to his desk, and for every good behavior I would mark an X in an additional square. It wasn't long before I noticed a child doodling, filling in the squares with X's. I realized immediately that this system wouldn't work, so I began to use IBM cards. The children remarked that they liked the cards better than the graphs because the cards were just like getting money. The graph marks were as negotiable as the cards, but children like to feel and collect something tangible. It's much more reinforcing.

Miss Bass, a primary teacher on Detroit's East Side, was having a great deal of difficulty managing her class. I did a demonstration lesson for her using tokens and positive reinforcement. The thirty-five students worked very hard and completed their assignments in record time. Miss Bass was fascinated and wanted to use the token system right away. I watched as she taught another lesson using positive reinforcement with tokens. She did quite well.

Two days later Miss Bass called for help. When I arrived, I found that the children did in fact have tokens, but Miss Bass was right when she said they were not working! Each child had literally hundreds of tokens which were so small they had to keep them in paper cups. Miss Bass was economy minded and wished to save paper. Her tokens were about one-half inch wide and one inch long. They were flimsy, hard to handle, and stuck together. A paper cup full of these tokens had no value. They were everywhere for the taking, and Miss Bass was waiting till the end of the week for the children to spend them.

If Miss Bass had used much larger paper, distributed the tokens only one at a time, and let the children spend them more often, she would have had no problem with the system.

The reason we recommend using tokens is that they provide a very convenient and immediate means for rewarding good behavior or the achievement of a learning task. Tokens provide concrete recognition, a tangible means of positive reinforcement. They also remind you, the teacher, to "be positive," to watch for good performance. And the tokens, because they are freely negotiable, give the student the opportunity to redeem them for various things which he can choose for himself.

Distributing the Tokens

Generally speaking, tokens should be given out one at a time. But if a student does ten times the work he is assigned, there is no reason why he shouldn't be given ten tokens. While teaching the class or helping individuals, you can carry a pack of cards or a handful of tokens and distribute them for observance of the rules, politeness, promptness, industry, improvement of any kind, thoughtfulness or respect for others, good papers, or for anything you think deserves recognition and reward.

You will want to reinforce the children for all kinds of good behavior and good performance, but not always for the same things. If you give praise and tokens spontaneously for all kinds of positive performance this way, you will maintain a good level of behavior and students will learn that any kind of good behavior is likely to "pay off."

It will be good at the beginning of the year to concentrate on reinforcing the students for their observance of the class Ground Rules. This will immediately create a good atmosphere for study and learning. But once this is established, you should gradually change your emphasis from the observance of rules to the achievement of learning tasks. With the contingency contracting you can give tokens for completing assignments, for accuracy, for neat work, and for extra credit projects.

As you get on into the school year, your tendency may be to give fewer tokens. Resist this. Giving tokens for good behavior and especially for the achievement of learning tasks keeps a positive atmosphere in your class, gives the students an earning power, and motivates them to good study habits.

Redeeming the Tokens

Tokens give the youngsters a purchasing power which they should be able to exercise fairly frequently. For small children and for older ones too, it is too long a time to have to wait until the end of the week to redeem their tokens. In general, the more immediate the reward the better.

Tokens can be spent for a variety of things depending upon your budget, your ingenuity, and especially upon the students' own preferences.

For instance, items for purchase. You might set up a shelf or a small "store" in your room where students can redeem their tokens for candy, trinkets, small gifts, or paperback books.

The tokens might be spent for ordinary small privileges like free time, listening to tapes, using filmstrips or learning machines, getting a drink of water, writing on the chalkboard instead of on paper, walking around the room, and a hundred other things that students like to do.

The tokens might also be used to "pay" for field trips, picnics, or the privilege of doing classroom tasks the students like to do for you--dusting the room, cleaning erasers, watering the plants, caring for pets. In one school where I taught the privilege the children desired most was that of carrying the bus driver's lunch for him.

It is very helpful for the behavior management system we are recommending to set aside a definite area of the classroom as a reinforcing events (RE) place, a "fun and games" area where the students can redeem their tokens for activities or items of their choice. Having an RE place is a convenient way of separating task events from reinforcing events. A room divider, bookcase, file cabinet, or even a tape on the floor can be enough to designate an RE area.

When several or all of the classes in the school participate in a token economy system, an RE room is very helpful, almost essential.

When a special RE room is used, the "store" and recreational facilities are located there. The tokens are the only medium of exchange for candy, pop, games, books, trinkets, and privileges. Certain items can be rented; for instance, the use of the ping-pong table or electric football game.

Students should have a definite period of time when they are allowed to go to the RE place. Two schools I have worked with where all the classes were involved in the token economy system both provided a definite time each week when students were allowed free time in the RE room. They would go as a class to enjoy the benefits of their work. In addition, an individual student could go to the RE room whenever he completed his work satisfactorily and his teacher felt he deserved a reward. A small number of tokens were required as an admission price. The RE room was managed by volunteer mothers.

When setting up a "store" for the first time, it is important to ask the students for suggestions. Remember that adult tastes and young people's tastes are widely different. The reinforcements are for the students; they have to be things that the students like. A committee of students might help stock the "store" and regulate the prices of things.

The value of a single token can vary, but it seems that students usually equate one token with one cent. They resent having to pay 150 tokens for a candy bar. If you have an RE place in your own classroom, you can determine the value of the token according to your own conditions and supplies.

A Sample Case

After I had been teaching intermediate level classes for about twelve years, I was faced with a group of fourth graders who had a consistent history of disruptive behavior. As soon as I began working with them, it became obvious that discipline, however severe, would have no real effect. So I planned a program of behavior management with tokens as incentives. I arranged a meeting with the children's parents and proposed a bold, innovative plan to create an orderly atmosphere in which learning could take place. A quick survey of the students had indicated that each one received about three dollars a week spending money from his parents. If the parents would agree to contribute half the student's allowance, $1.50 per week, for reinforcements for good behavior and good performance, I would introduce a token-reward system in which the students could redeem their tokens for various items in a "store." When I promised that behavior problems would diminish and grades would improve, the parents agreed to give the system a try for one semester.

With the money contributed I bought candy, books, toys, records, and games which the children could buy or rent with their tokens. They could also use the tokens to pay for special privileges around school or to pay for field trips.

After about two months an interesting thing happened. The candy and toys lost their attraction, and the students were more interested in saving their tokens for privileges or for field trips. A potential problem became a valuable learning experience when I asked the students themselves to propose ways for spending the tokens. What did they want?

First of all, they wanted to pay to use equipment in the classroom such as the record player, the tape recorder, or the chalkboard. Secondly, some wished to be "teacher" and to correct papers or help other students. Others wanted to put on plays for other classes.

By taking your cues from the students, you can evolve a very successful reinforcement system.

How much does it cost to set up an RE program in a school? One school with 450 students spent a little more than eighty dollars for their whole program, the proceeds from a bake sale. Another school of about the same size prepared a budget for a year-long behavior management program and estimated the cost at one and one-half cents per child per day. This proved more than adequate. Another school I consulted with had ten thousand dollars to spend for the year on reinforcements. The amount of the budget and the success of the program do not necessarily go together. The two schools with smaller budgets had very elaborate and very successful programs. The school with the large budget did too.

When the budget is small, students have to have ways to spend tokens on non-consumable items. It is best to have store items which the children can actually keep, but this is not essential. The program will work very well with items that can be rented. Tokens may also be spent on field trips, parties, contests, free time, privileges, and special events. Once again, ask the students what they like and what they would like to do. It is their program. They know best what they find rewarding.

Parent Involvement

Parent understanding and involvement are essential to the success of any behavior management program. Positive reinforcement and a token economy system are probably foreign to most parents, so a short orientation meeting or two is important. The great majority of parents are vitally interested and eager to help with their children's education. The more they can be involved in recognizing and praising the achievements of their children, the better the program will be.

The RE room at St. Bride's School on Chicago's South Side was managed and staffed entirely by volunteer mothers. They contributed over fifteen hundred hours of service throughout the year. Thompson School in Highland Park, Michigan totaled 850 volunteer hours from November 1 to May 10. These hours of contributed service were computed by the current minimum wage, and the total contribution with the names of each volunteer mother was tallied and published in the school bulletin. This provided a very visible and gratifying reinforcement for the parents' involvement in the school.

Tokens and Freedom

One of the most important things we teachers have to do is give the students a chance to choose for themselves. Making choices is an important part of the maturing process. If we make all the decisions, or even most of them, the students develop an unhealthy dependence on us. When a student asks permission to do something, we can let him evaluate the situation and make his own decision.

Charles was in junior high and felt that tokens were beneath him. He wanted a more sophisticated method for handling our pseudo-money system. He wanted a checkbook system instead of the tokens.

We could have responded in one of two ways. We could have said, "No, Charlie, this is the best way to run a token economy." Or we could have said, "That sounds like a good idea, Charles; why not get a committee together and work out a better plan?"

We choose the second way.

A few days later, the committee decided that our token system was the best for our circumstances because without an elaborate school-wide banking system no one would be able to tell for sure how much "money" there actually was in each account. There was the added difficulty that the small children involved in the program would not be able to write checks or understand the banking system.

If we had said, "No, the checkbooks won't work!" we would have had a lot of grumbling and discontent. But because we said "Yes," we were on the students' side, respected their abilities, and taught them how to think through a problem and come up with a decision on their own.

Students need and want this kind of freedom, free choice

within reasonable alternatives. They want the right to find out for themselves, but they need direction, and they also need support. Teachers who deny this kind of freedom are much too fearful of losing control.

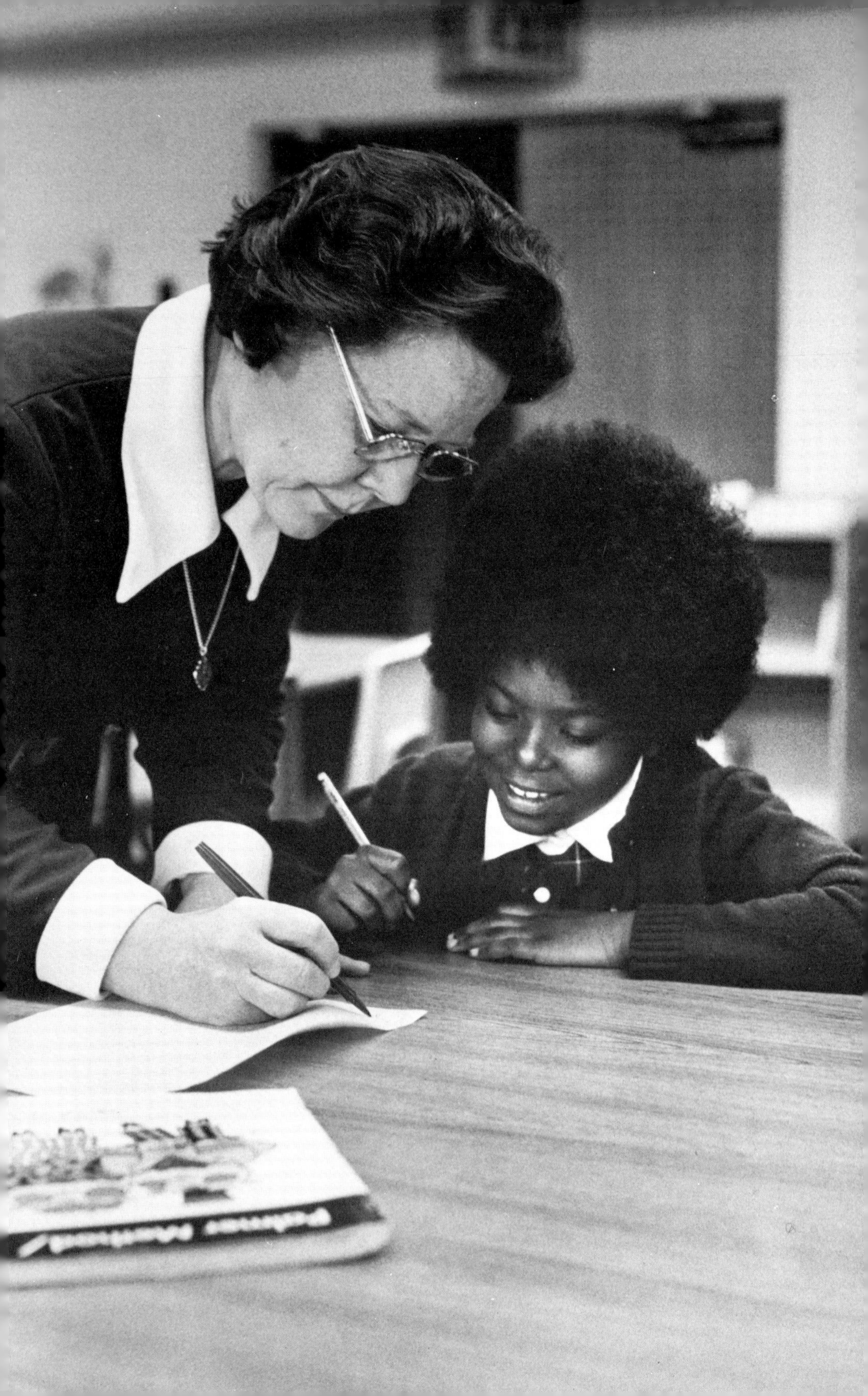

6

Helps for Learning

A student's learning will be as efficient and effective as his motivation to learn. Your task as the teacher will be to discover what most effectively motivates each student and then couple or contract that motivator with the immediate learning situation. Praise and recognition helps everyone. Some need tactile assurance too. Others will be motivated by tokens and tangible rewards. And still others can work for the joy of learning.

Each student is differently motivated, and the general principle is that the student himself knows best what is reinforcing to him at any given time. The purpose of this chapter will simply be to describe some different types of rewards that are likely to be reinforcing to different students. You will have to supplement our initial proposals with those from your own experience.

Praise and Recognition

The basic idea underlying this whole book is that praise is

very reinforcing to students. Verbal recognition is often enough to satisfy most students. Everyone thrives on love and attention.

Rita and Jeanne were twins in kindergarten when we first met. Their similarity ended with their appearance, however, because their personalities were markedly different. Rita was quite self-sufficient and needed only the verbal recognition of her teacher. Jeanne needed more dramatic assurances of approval. She thrived on her teacher's hugs and pats on the head.

It will be very helpful to brief the students' parents on your positive teaching plan and involve them in it as much as possible. Encourage them to ask the student regularly how he is doing in school, have them praise him for his efforts and reward him in a personal way for his progress and achievements.

One school we worked in asked each teacher to call or write a note once a week to the parents of the child who showed the most improvement that week. The parents were amazed and pleasantly surprised. They only expect to hear from the teacher when there's a problem.

Ways to praise:

Displaying papers and other good work in the classroom
Reading aloud in class
Demonstration to class or visitors
Phone call to parents to praise good work

Tokens and Tangible Rewards

Our last chapter described how to set up a token economy system. The power to earn tokens is very reinforcing for most students. It will be enough to point out here that tokens should be given immediately upon completion of the desirable behavior or learning task, the student should know why he is being rewarded, and it is best if the student can redeem his tokens or purchase something with them fairly soon after he has earned them.

Purchase items in RE place:

Candy
Soda pop
Paperback books
Gifts
School supplies

Rental items in RE place:

Games
Use of science equipment
Use of tape recorder
Use of record player, stories or music
TV

Preferred Subjects and Activities

If you know your students well, you can use preferred activities or even preferred studies to motivate the youngsters.

Delina was a second grader who loved to read. She was the type of child who had to have a book close at hand even when she was taking a bath. Delina needed no other reinforcement than the privilege of being able to read. I could say to her, "Delina, as soon as you answer the questions on this social studies unit, you may read whatever you wish for the next half hour."

With interesting material, certain learning activities can be reinforcers for less interesting study tasks. Students in a fourth grade class paid tokens to do advanced science using the World Book Cyclo-teacher. They would work to finish an assignment, be paid tokens when they completed the task, then use the tokens in different ways. Some saved them for store time at the end of the day. Others would spend them immediately to listen to the tape recorder or record player with earphones. And some would spend them to use the Cyclo-teacher or do an additional assignment in a subject of their choice. The additional work if done well could earn three or four times as many tokens as it cost to do the initial assignment. It did not take long for the students to become astute financiers. This is a great way to teach elements of our economy.

To repeat, working on preferred subjects can be made contingent upon the completion of less agreeable school work. Jack loved chemistry and hated mathematics. But as soon as it became clear to him that he needed the math in order to do the chemistry, he worked very hard at the numbers. He worked harder than he or anyone else would have believed and eventually he won a high school scholarship in math.

It might work just the other way around, of course. Another student who loves math and hates literature might be motivated to read short stories with the prospect of having time to work on his figures when he read the stories.

Children who find academic subjects very difficult might be helped to work through them by the hope of having time to work on art projects or to color the outlines on a geopolitical map. Sensitive teachers will capitalize on this kind of expertise in a student. We generally put too little emphasis on manual dexterity.

Many schools recognize that the privilege of playing on an athletic team is a powerful reinforcer. They require that students have a B or C average in their studies in order to play on the teams.

Some preferred activities and studies:

As you work with a token reward system, you will notice a certain evolution in the things the students prefer as rewards. Candy and soda pop will probably be much in demand at the beginning, but then paperback books, if you can furnish an attractive selection, will become more desirable as time goes on. One school responded to this by adding a learning resource center across the hall from the "fun and games" RE room. The students paid a few tokens for admission to both rooms, and the learning center gradually grew in popularity.

Adult Relationships

Relationships with teachers, paraprofessionals, counsellors, and other staff people, are definitely reinforcing to many students.

Most of the school staff thought Dennis was a "bad" boy. He was always the prime candidate for the counsellor, social worker, or psychologist, whoever was working in the school that day. Dennis related beautifully to the adult worker in a one-to-one situation. But as soon as he got back to the classroom, he would harass the teacher and the other students. It was not until late in the year that I was asked to consult with the other professionals about Dennis.

At the age of seven Dennis had five adults giving him sympathy, encouragement, candy, and a whole lot of attention. At this rate, Dennis spent several hours a week outside his classroom. The pattern was the same every time. Dennis would respond positively to the professional, then return to his classroom a devil-on-wheels.

The adults could not understand why Dennis was not responding to all the help he was getting. As a behavior consultant I simply suggested that Dennis had a good thing going for him. He had learned to manipulate the adults. He knew that if he were "bad," his teacher would send him to see the counsellor. He also knew that he could play up to the counsellor by promising to try harder to be good.

I suggested that Dennis' visits to the professionals be made contingent upon appropriate behavior for a specified time in the classroom.

Although Dennis' acting up had continued unabated through two years of counselling by various professionals, the five consultants were divided in their reaction to my contingency plan. Some were enthusiastic, others thought the boy should have access to the counsellor whenever he felt it was necessary.

I resisted this latter position and asked for a two-week trial period to show that Dennis was actually manipulating them. They agreed to the trial period.

As soon as possible Dennis, his teacher, and I met to set up some rules. Dennis was to see his speech therapist only after he completed his first assignment on Thursday mornings. He could see the social worker if he earned four tokens for being polite to his teacher on Tuesdays. Dennis had to earn every meeting he had with an adult outside the classroom.

The school year ended before we could adequately judge the success of Dennis' program. But for the last few weeks of school, his teacher did find that he was much less of a problem to her and to the other children in the class. In fact, she thought she was beginning to like Dennis rather than tolerate him.

The point is that relationships with adults are very welcome, valuable, and reinforcing for young people. The possibility of beginning or fostering such a relationship might be a powerful incentive for good behavior or for working through certain learning tasks.

The Joy of Learning

There is a sense in which tokens and tangible rewards, the privilege of choosing preferred activities, field trips, and even praise and recognition are external motivators. This is not to say that they are any the less good or effective. (How much work would we do if we were not paid?) But there is a goal which we teachers can aim at and try to direct our students toward, and that is the point at which the student discovers a joy in learning, the point at which insight and knowledge become their own reward.

    The joy of learning can be very reinforcing in itself. We have all experienced it at one time or another ourselves. We have seen children delight in achievement or mastery. We have seen older students take pride in the joy of discovery. This is a precious and delicate moment. The teacher who can guide the student toward it is a master. And the wise teacher will know instinctively that when a student approaches this point, he or she must stand back and let the student go on his own. Praise and encouragement are fine, but all other motivators will be unnecessary, and any controls will be a hindrance. When the student gets "turned on" to learning, encourage him, suggest resources and materials, and give him all the freedom you can to pursue his interest and curiosity.

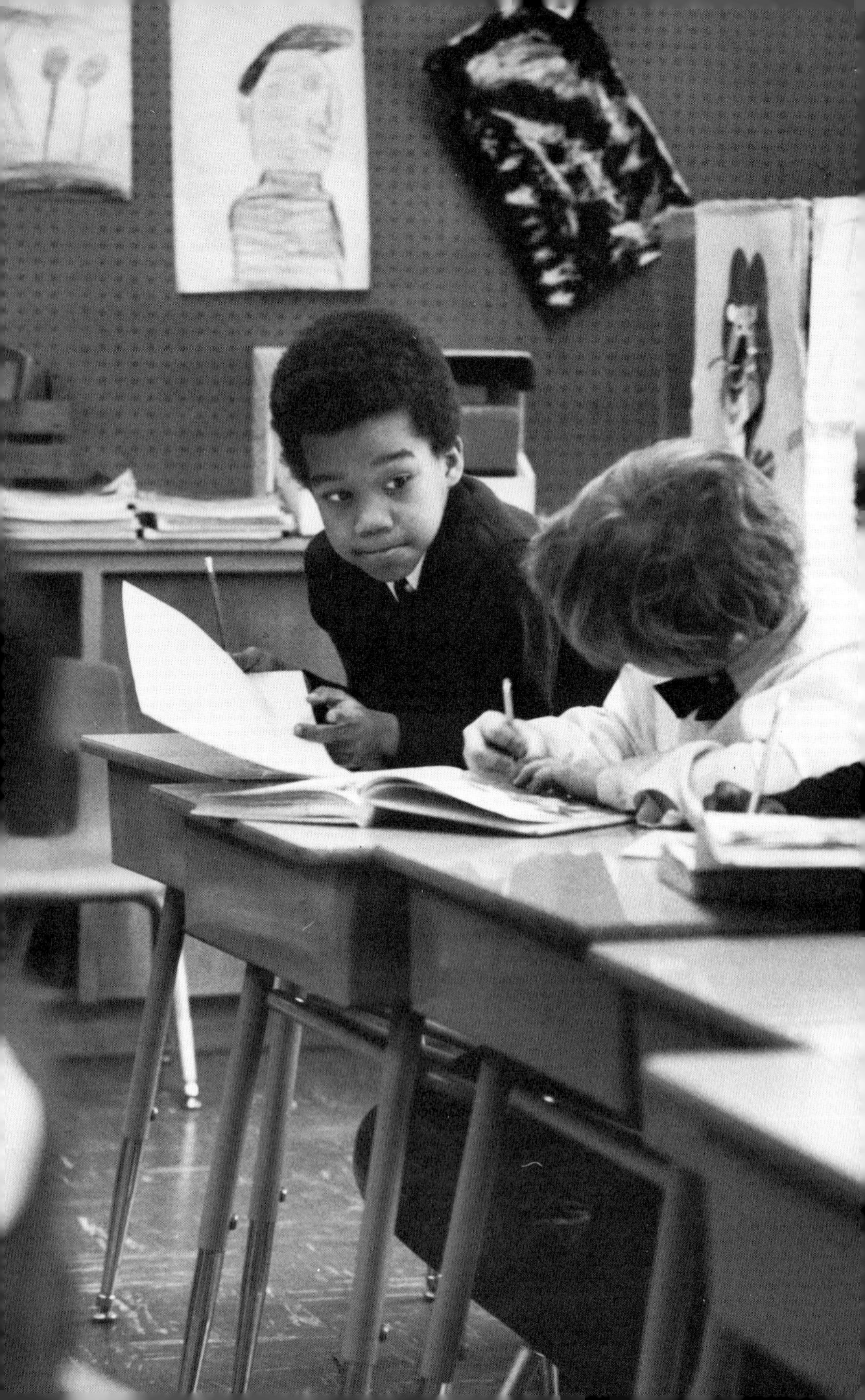

7

Problems and Discipline

Deviant behavior occurs in every material organism, in every human situation, in every classroom. Students who act out-of-order do so for reasons which can be discovered and analyzed. The problem may be in the teacher, the classroom environment, the teacher-student relationship, the student's need for attention, inappropriate subject matter, or a variety of other things. If we observe behavior closely and analyze it, we can change it.

Mrs. Anderson's Class

Mrs. Anderson asked us to observe her class because she felt that all of her students were either retarded or emotionally disturbed. She felt that the principal had given her all the worst kids in the school. Upon investigation we discovered that Mrs. Anderson was entirely serious in her judgments. She would say to us in a voice loud enough for the students to hear, "See, they are crazy; they talk to themselves. They never listen to me. They always do as they please. I just don't think they belong in a regular class. They need to be in special education!"

The students did indeed talk to themselves. They had a good role model in Mrs. Anderson. They also did exactly as they pleased. They had long since given up trying to interpret her directives.

Mrs. Anderson's students were between the ages of six and eight. They were in a transition group, which meant that they had had one year of kindergarten but were not yet ready for first grade. There were fifteen students in the class.

Mrs. Anderson told us that after recess the class was at its worst. This is when we went to observe them. There were many problems. During the first thirty minutes of our observation Mrs. Anderson made 109 remarks that were irrelevant to the lesson she was teaching. (This did not include legitimate academic directions.)

On the second day we observed her class, Mrs. Anderson made thirty-one irrelevant remarks, but she spent a total of twenty minutes at the door talking with another teacher whose class was at the water fountain. Mrs. A. would occasionally interrupt her conversation long enough to shout into the room, "Daniel, be nice." Or, "Michael, don't do that!"

On the third day we arranged for a closed circuit television camera to record Mrs. Anderson and her class in action. We gave no special instructions to Mrs. A. We only asked her permission to videotape the class.

During this thirty-minute session, Mrs. Anderson tried to act in a more traditional way; she flitted around the room giving a lot of attention to children who were running about or playing. Between smiling into the camera and talking with the consultants, Mrs. Anderson tried to attend to the work some of the children were doing.

It was becoming clear that Mrs. Anderson was the cause of the deviant behavior in her classroom.

When we sat down with Mrs. Anderson and replayed the videotape, we pointed out that during the three periods which we observed, six children attended to their work 100 percent of the time, and yet their names were not mentioned once, nor was their work recognized.

Our meeting seemed satisfactory because Mrs. Anderson very much wanted to be a good teacher. She was willing to try harder.

We agreed to do a classroom demonstration lesson to show her how tokens and consistent behavior on her part would help eliminate some of the problems she was having.

This public school had no financial surplus to allow for even a small "store" or RE room, so we gathered together all the "fun" things in the classroom itself and placed them on a table behind the piano. This became the RE area.

As the children earned tokens for appropriate behavior, they could trade them for time in the RE area. It took the class all of about three minutes to discover that children who were sitting and working were getting "something." For thirty minutes the children worked quietly and diligently completing a handwriting and number assignment.

As each child finished his paper, he was given an egg timer to spend three minutes in the RE area reading books, playing with clay, coloring, or just looking out the window. At the end of the three minute period, the child returned to his desk where we gave him individual attention and instruction for completing another paper with recess as his goal. Each child was praised and was given tokens for working hard and completing his lessons.

So this solved everything? Well, not quite.

After the first two papers a child, let's call him Leo, threw his papers, pencils, and crayons on the floor and shouted that he was not going to do the _____ work!

We ignored Leo and continued to praise the children who were working. Leo then opened his desk and began to throw more papers and books on the floor. All the while he mumbled under his breath. He cursed the school, the teacher, his parents, and even the principal. He fully expected to be sent to the principal for a paddling.

We continued to ignore Leo and his antics. Leo wanted attention very badly. It was recess time and as each child finished his work, we allowed him to go out to recess. In a short time all of the students were out of the room but Leo. We told him that as soon as his paper was finished and he picked up his papers and books, he could go to recess, but not before.

When recess was over, Leo was more determined than ever not to do his work. We found out later that recess was a punishing experience for him because he was not well-liked by his classmates and they frequently picked on him. It was necessary at this point to make the tokens as appealing as possible by having them immediately negotiable for a treat outside the class.

Children like free time. So in giving the class instructions for completing the next assignment we said, "When you finish your paper, you will have earned three tokens which you can spend for free time if you wish. You can do any kind of school activity you want to. You may go to the library or watch TV or read books; you may go out and get a drink, or write on the chalkboard, or go to the RE area.

At this point Leo stood up and threw his chair across the room.

Time Out

This called for the Time Out procedure. We took belligerent Leo by the hand and gently led him down the hall to the principal's office. Mr. Murphy, the principal, had agreed to cooperate with our procedure. Time Out is a period of quiet away from anyone who can give attention in a place where the culprit cannot earn any tokens. Leo was to sit in a small annex to Mr. Murphy's office. The room was bare, no windows. Leo was told he would have to sit there until he felt ready to return to class, pick up the papers he threw on the floor, and do his work.

This was about ten-thirty in the morning. Mr. Murphy ignored Leo, but used an outside phone to call his mother and tell her about Leo's episode and the tactics that were now being used with him. She was fully cooperative and agreed that Leo could be kept through lunch if necessary.

About two o'clock in the afternoon Leo had had enough Time Out and asked if he might return to his classroom. He said he was sorry and promised to be good and do his work. "What else?" asked Mr. Murphy. "I will pick up the books and papers," said Leo.

When Leo returned to the classroom, we paid no attention to him until he had begun to work. Then we said, "Leo, you're doing fine. Keep up the good work."

This ended the episode. We ignored Leo's acting out as long as possible, but when it appeared that he might injure someone by throwing the chair, we put him in Time Out. Attention of any kind, especially talking to, reasoning with, looking at, shaming or spanking, is rewarding. Time Out deprives the student of attention and thus is the best corrective.

If serious misbehavior occurs and you cannot put the disruptive child in a room by himself, then you can establish a Time Out place in your own classroom. With a designated place off in a corner, you can give Patrick five minutes of Time Out when he is not allowed to earn tokens nor is he given any attention.

Raising your voice and scolding the child makes him stop his disruptive behavior for the moment, but it has no lasting effect. Time Out makes a student responsible for his actions. He disobeyed a rule, so for five or ten minutes his earning power is limited. His is not attacked as a person. Rather his act is punished.

A Word About Punishment

Nagging, scolding, spanking, and all kinds of physical punishment are the least effective disciplinary procedures. This kind of punishment appears to be effective because it momentarily suppresses misbehavior. This is why yelling at students is a common practice. But yelling only creates hostility and the desire to escape a bad situation. It only makes the student avoid the act in your presence. He may very well throw the eraser or punch Johnny when you are not looking.

When David is turned around and engrossed in conversation with the student behind him, your shouting his name will abruptly get him back to work. But the minute you turn your head, he may continue his conversation. This time with the added challenge of escaping your attention. No matter what happens, though, David has gotten a great deal of attention for the wrong things.

This kind of discipline pays attention to inappropriate behavior and reinforces it. Some students find the notoriety of being punished this way much more desirable than the oblivion usually accorded those who are good. Tape record yourself for thirty minutes and find out whether inappropriate behavior "pays off" for your students this way. Disruptive behavior is usually cited three-to-one over good behavior. Most teachers, like most people, tend to pay attention to bad conduct and ignore the good. As we have said before, this reinforces the disruptive and weakens the good behavior patterns.

Constantly reminding or nagging children is the most ineffective way to change their behavior. It is punishing, too, because it insults the child's intelligence and does not allow him to be responsible for his own actions. Take Phyllis for instance.

Phyllis was reluctant to get out of bed in the morning. Her mother very much wanted her to be on time for the school bus. If Phyllis missed the bus, her mother would drive her to school, an extra trip in the car.

Every night before bed Phyllis would get the same sermon about rising on time, being cooperative, not being an inconvenience to others, and so on. Every night Phyllis would mumble under her breath that she was being persecuted, her mother hated her, and so on, and so on.

Every morning Phyllis would hear her mother call and

she'd just turn over and burrow deeper under the covers. The calling would continue for about an hour. Everyone became more irritated and aggravated with each call. And when Phyllis finally got up, she would be angry, not a good way to begin the school day.

We met Phyllis' mother at a conference where we spoke about how parents might use contingency contracting at home. Mrs. Johnson approached us after the meeting to ask for some specific advice in dealing with Phyllis. We suggested that she buy Phyllis an alarm clock. They should then sit down together and discuss the situation. First of all, Phyllis would have to decide how much time she needed to get ready for school in the morning. If she missed the bus, she would either walk to school, ride her bike, or stay home. The family car would no longer provide taxi service. For each day that Phyllis made the bus, she would be given one-fifth of her allowance. Any day that she remained at home she would work as closely as possible to the school schedule. She would read, write, or study in her room, and only after the usual dismissal time could she go out and do as she pleased. If Phyllis missed two days of school in the same week, she agreed to forego the privilege of going out with her friends on the weekend. These agreements were written out in a formal contract and signed by Phyllis and her parents.

The first morning Phyllis allowed herself one-half hour to dress, eat breakfast, and catch the bus. Mrs. Johnson was awake in bed but steadfastly resisted calling her daughter. The alarm rang and Phyllis answered it immediately. But one-half hour was not enough. The bus arrived a little early and Phyllis missed it. She stayed at home and kept to the regular school schedule.

For the rest of the week everything went well. Phyllis got up and made the bus every day. But one night the following week, Phyllis forgot to set the alarm. She overslept the next morning, but her mother did not call her. Phyllis stayed home, read her textbooks for part of the morning, and started to watch TV around noon. Mrs. Johnson simply said, "The contract calls for you to study in your room until two-fifty this afternoon." Phyllis turned off the TV and returned to her room.

Two days later Phyllis again overslept. This time, however, she raced to get dressed and walked the mile and a half to school. She didn't want to miss a second day and be grounded on the weekend. This was Homecoming Week.

Phyllis and Mrs. Johnson no longer have their early-morning battle. Phyllis feels that her mother is nicer because she doesn't nag. Mrs. Johnson is happy because Phyllis assumes much more responsibility.

A specific program, contingent rewards, and consistent management of the agreement solved the problem. Mrs. Johnson could change her own behavior and help her daughter assume the responsibility of changing hers.

There may be a time when you will be faced with out-and-out conflict in the classroom, the danger of serious injury, or a major challenge to authority. This sort of thing cannot be ignored. It must be handled immediately and effectively, but in a way that will give the student the least amount of attention. This is why we recommend the Time Out procedure. It removes the student briefly from the scene of the trouble, he is not insulted, and the problem is resolved with the least amount of disturbance.

One reason why students argue with their teachers is because it will get them attention and response. If a conflict situation like this arises in your class, be calm. When the student has finished, invite him to make an appointment with you or the principal for further discussion after class. This way you refuse to join the conflict, no one loses face, and you can continue to be a teacher. Other students wish to be taught.

When you have a student who is acting out, it is best to use a calm, non-threatening voice. Do not attack him, rather point out briefly that his behavior is contrary to the class rules which he helped to form. Nine times out of ten this approach will work. But if you raise your voice and threaten a student or push him to the wall, he has only one way to go, and that is to come out fighting. If you remain calm, you prove that you cannot be easily ruffled and the students will no longer try to challenge you in this way.

It is best, of course, to defuse a conflict with the least possible disturbance right in the classroom. If you overreact, respond in anger, have a student suspended, or call in the principal, it may give the culprit a feeling of victory. He forced you to make a drastic move. He becomes a hero to his peers because he stood up to the teacher.

When a student is sent to the principal's office, he gets a lot of attention for being bad. It might be enough to quietly ask him to sit somewhere else in the room. In one Chicago school, the principal's office was turned into a rewarding place. The children who were exceptionally good were sent to the principal for additional praise and recognition.

If it has to be used at all, be sure your punishment fits the crime. The punishment exceeds the crime when a student is suspended from school for throwing pencils, erasers, or paper. It would be much better to have the youngster sweep the classroom and dust it, or possibly pick up papers from the school yard.

When a teacher orders a child of six to write "I shall not talk" five hundred times, the punishment is far worse than the crime. Excessively severe punishments such as "no recess for the rest of the year" are also unreasonable and ineffective. The child has no hope of completing the punishment.

Serious misbehavior calls for a serious response. If you merely respond with warnings, accusations, or empty threats, the situation will surely get worse.

Consistency is essential. Clear rules. Perhaps a reminder. Then reasonable penalties for clear violations which cannot be ignored. Use a calm voice and say, "Charlie, the rule is . . . Since you have broken the rule repeatedly, you will have to spend five minutes in Time Out."

Mrs. Kerns found Burton chewing gum and told him to put it on the end of his nose until recess. The whole class laughed and guffawed and ridiculed Burton until he cried.

Mr. Adams noticed Steven secretly blowing a bubble. He called Steve out into the hall and talked to him about gum chewing in school. Mr. Adams told the boy he'd have to stay after school for a punishment. Later in the day Steven was again caught chewing gum. Since he already had to stay after school, he figured one more offense wouldn't make any difference.

Mr. Daniels saw Bill with gum in his mouth. Several others were chewing gum too. As the class was small, Mr. Daniels excused from homework every student who did not have gum in his mouth at the moment. This did not draw attention to Bill, but gave attention and a small reward to those who obeyed the school rule.

The point of this chapter is simply this; problems and deviant behavior are almost certain to occur in your classroom. When they do, remember to ignore the inappropriate behavior as much as possible while you positively reinforce the good behavior. Harmful or potentially injurious behavior which cannot be ignored should be handled with a Time Out procedure and with as little attention as possible. And remember, at all times, be fair and consistent.

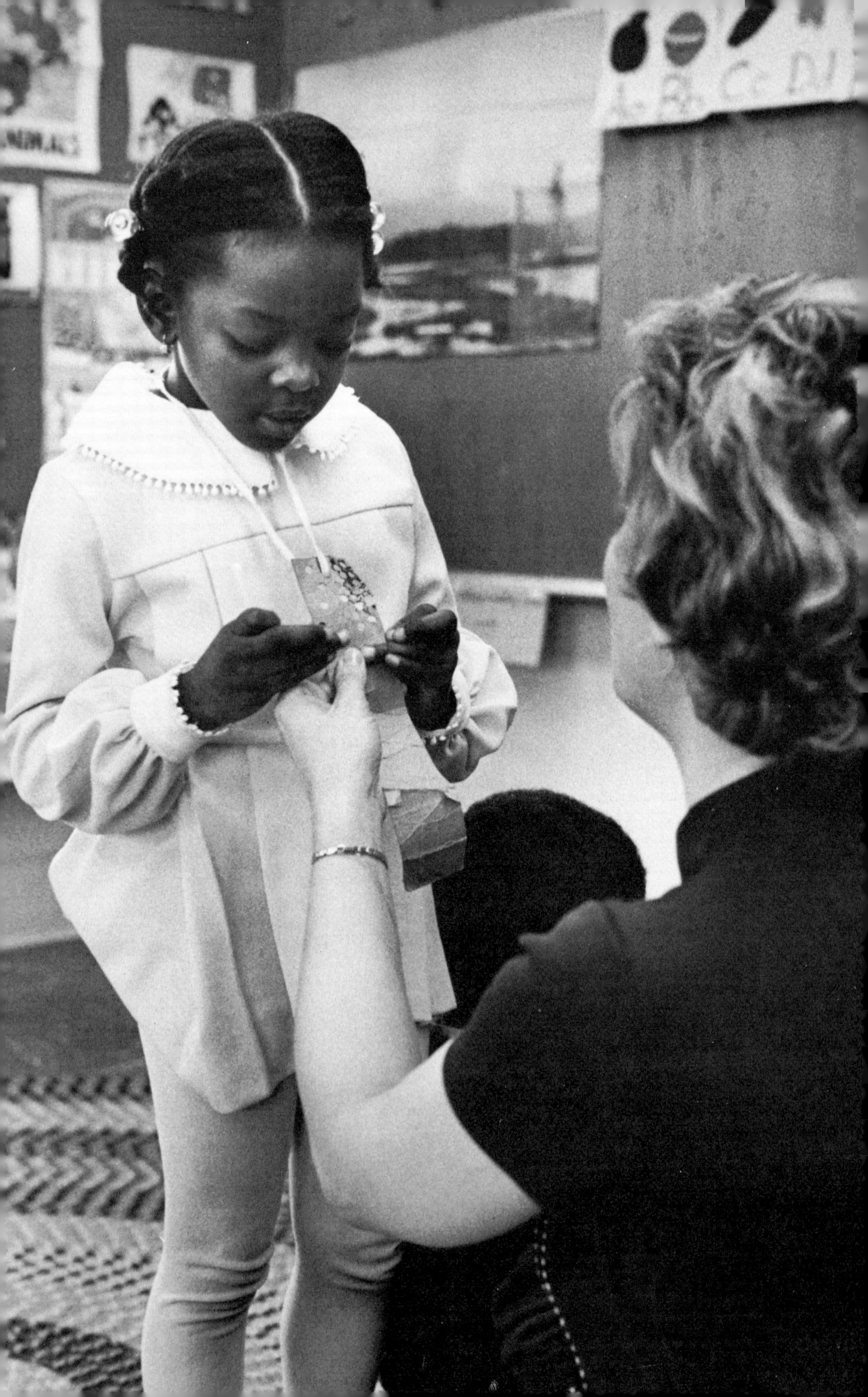

8

Shaping New Behavior

New behavior can very easily be shaped by allowing the student to choose something desirable that will serve as a reward for performing a specific learning task. If Nancy likes to talk to Connie, the two might be grouped together to share difficult learning tasks. Then Nancy may have free time to talk with Connie as soon as both finish their work.

By making a preferred activity contingent upon completion of a difficult learning task, the student has a motive, other than the teacher's directive, for doing what is difficult.

In shaping new behaviors, it is essential to reinforce initial attempts at the desired behavior. A student will gradually perform better and better if his small steps are praised and encouraged. It is a good idea to keep daily records on a student's progress. When a student has only to compete with himself, he does not have the fears and tensions of group competition. It is also very reinforcing for a student to see his own daily improvements. When a teacher pays attention to the small steps and praises his progress, the student gets attention for the right reasons.

Barbara needed a lot of encouragement and attention to counteract her personal insecurity. We first met Barbara when she was in the second grade. She had very little self-confidence at that time. In fact, she wouldn't even attempt an assignment for fear of failure.

We began by giving Barbara very small assignments with guaranteed, built-in success. Each segment was counted as a full assignment, graded, and charted on a graph. Barbara soon began to smile as she did her work because she knew it was going to be correct. She knew she could succeed. By mid-year Barbara was ready to do the same assignments as her classmates. She had received a lot of encouragement from her teacher. Her many small successes had built up her self-confidence.

It does not help a student to keep him in an easy work program too long. He needs a constant challenge, and eventually a chance to cope with failure. Insecure children cannot do this. Their self-confidence must first be built up to the point where a challenge is manageable, not defeating.

Another tip: be sure to tell the student why he is being rewarded. It does so much good to say, "Thank you, Lori, for working so hard. I am proud of you." This is the kind of remark a student will remember. It also serves as a cue to those who are not working quite so hard. Then you only have to watch and comment when the good behavior begins to pay off in better learning.

When you say to Lori, "I am proud of you for working so hard," the whole class sits up and works harder. Notice how different this is from the traditional negative approach of correcting and scolding. When the teacher said, "Delwin, stop that. Immediately!" Everyone stopped his work to look and see what Delwin was doing. The whole class was disrupted. But when you praise good behavior in one, you encourage good behavior in others. Students want to be noticed. If you recognize them for their good work, they will work a little harder.

When shaping new behavior, it is important to reinforce it every time it occurs. This will make the behavior habitual.

And once it is habitual, you can diminish the reinforcement gradually without eliminating it altogether.

We recommend that you begin by shaping behaviors which create an atmosphere for study before you try to shape study habits themselves. For instance, students often come into the classroom and talk or dally around so that the class starts anywhere from fifteen minutes to a half hour late. By simply reinforcing those students who come in, hang up their coats, and get their books ready for class, you can cut the dallying to a tolerable five or six minutes, time enough to collect the milk money!

We would recommend giving tokens to everyone in this way for several weeks, then gradually giving the tokens only to the first five or ten students who are prepared by a given time. Then maybe just to the first two who are ready. Continue to praise the class in general for their cooperation. Then find another behavior which needs to be shaped so that the students will have alternate ways to earn tokens. Once they begin to earn tokens, they like the idea, because each token means success or good work or approval, and children like all of these.

Once a behavior pattern, such as sitting quickly and preparing for class, becomes established, it can be maintained if it is reinforced only occasionally. But the same reinforcer, if given too much or too often, can become distasteful. Intermittant reinforcement of established behaviors is best. Occasional praise will be more sincere.

When reinforcements are given too much or too often, a student can be satiated. Jeremiah, a small boy, was finding reading very distasteful. While he was working with a teacher aide, Jerry was being reinforced with M&M's each time he wrote a correct answer. When Jerry got the first M&M, he put it into his mouth. But as the morning wore on, he collected the M&M's in a paper cup. Then he ate the "whole thing." As Jerry began to work again, the aide placed another M&M in Jerry's cup. Jerry looked up with large pleading eyes and said, "Please don't give me any more; I'll do my work."

Jerry had been satiated. The M&M's had lost their effect.

   Consistency and common sense combined with appropriate study materials should build a classroom atmosphere conducive to good teaching and good learning, good feelings and good self-concepts. And all of this leads to people with a love for learning.

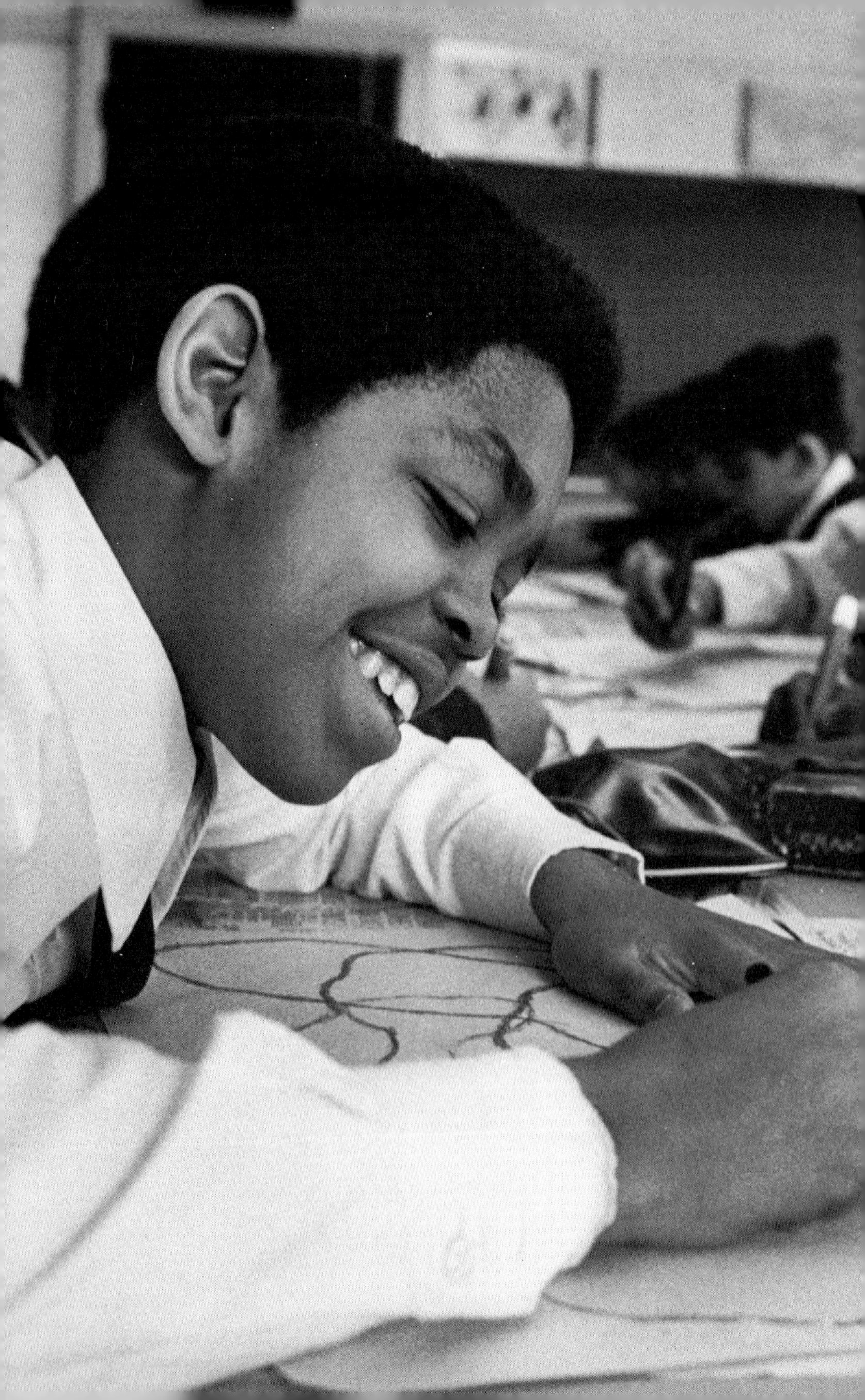

A
The SCAN Plan

One of the best examples we have seen of how contingency contracting and positive reinforcement can improve the learning situation occurred in the Cortland School in Highland Park, Michigan. The SCAN plan, as the program was called, was developed by Mrs. Louise Wilkerson under our guidance.

SCAN was born of a need. In mid-November we were asked to consult with Mrs. Wilkerson regarding the poor work habits of her fifth grade pupils. Many of these children were underachievers and some were behavior problems. There were twenty-eight children in the class.

Mrs. Wilkerson's students were submitting unfinished, untidy, unsigned, and incorrect papers. We proposed that four points be awarded for each assignment; one point each for the paper being Submitted, Complete, Accurate, and Neat. Every student in the class had the opportunity to earn at least three out of four points for papers that were submitted, complete, and neat. The accuracy point was also within easy reach because only a 70 percent passing grade was required to earn the additional accuracy point.

Each week Mrs. Wilkerson kept track of the total number of points which could be earned. Those students who earned 70 percent of the possible points for the week became members of a special group called a Citizenship Council. The members of the Council got a special privilege every Friday afternoon. One week the privilege was a field trip, the second week a bingo game, the third week a movie, and the fourth week a party.

The success of the SCAN plan can be seen on the graph on page 83. On November 23 six students made the Council. The reward that week was a mini field trip to the consultants' office one block from school. The office staff was highly reinforcing to the six Council members. Since our agency dealt with school referrals, there were many games and books for children in the office. Staff members interrupted their work to give individual attention to each child.

The following week, November 30, there were only two additional students eligible for the Council, but the class average rose from 49 to 63.9 percent. Almost two-thirds of the class were now submitting neat, completed assignments. These Council members asked for the same privilege, to visit the consultants' office again.

A special contract was made at the beginning of the third week. All those who made the Council could go to Cobo Hall for the Winter Carnival. This week twenty-five of the twenty-eight students in the class made the Council. But Mrs. Wilkerson made a tactical error. She let the three students make up their work at the last minute and allowed them to go to Cobo Hall with the Council members. For the next several weeks, these three students consistently did not make the Council. But by that time Mrs. Wilkerson had become consistent and the three missed the Friday afternoon privileges including a big adventure to Cranbrook Institute. They had gambled and lost. But they soon got down to work, made the Council, and enjoyed its privileges.

During the week of December 14, the Council membership fell off drastically because there were parent-teacher

Weekly Progress Chart for SCAN Plan

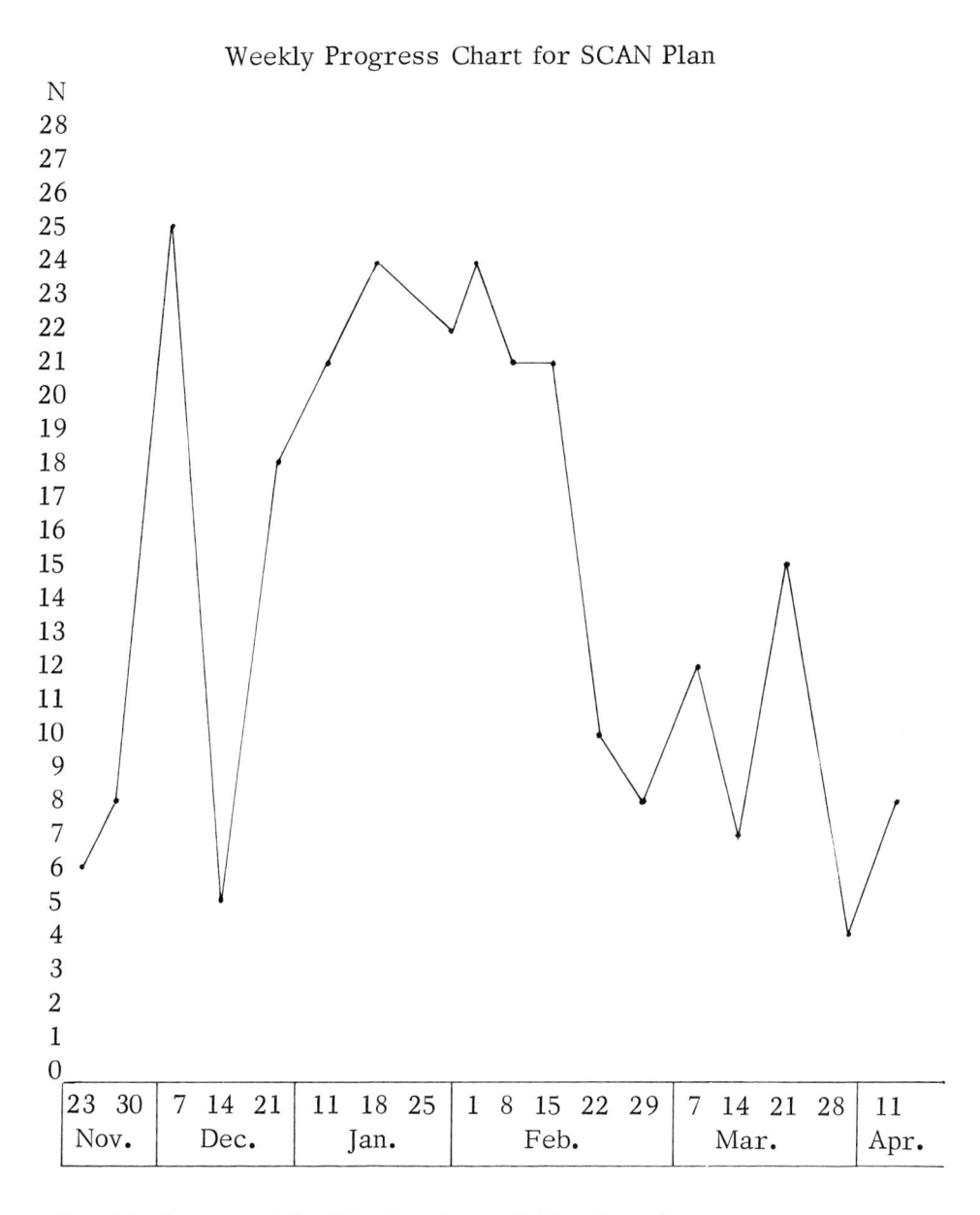

23 30	7 14 21	11 18 25	1 8 15 22 29	7 14 21 28	11
Nov.	Dec.	Jan.	Feb.	Mar.	Apr.

N - 28 Students Eligible for Council Membership

conferences for three half-days and Mrs. Wilkerson was absent for two days. Only five students made the Council that week and the class average fell to 59 percent. The Council membership was still two above the first week which indicated that some positive work habits were being formed.

The following week, December 21, a traditionally "bad" week before Christmas, there were eighteen Council members and the class average was 73 percent. In effect, almost three-fourths of the students were submitting completed, neat, and accurate assignments. The graph shows how the Council membership held good until the week of February 22 when two factors changed at the same time. First, the requirement for Council membership was raised from 70 to 80 percent (probably an error in view of the second change). And secondly, a new student teacher began teaching the class.

The student teacher had a markedly different approach to the children. As a result, inconsistency became the rule rather than the exception. During the first eleven weeks of the SCAN program, the students worked hard to become members of the Council. Except for the week of December 14, the SCAN plan was efficient. It set out specific attainable goals and furnished desirable, relatively immediate rewards for achieving them. But when teacher performance became inconsistent and the requirements for Council membership were raised at the same time, student progress began to falter.

For the remainder of the school year, student placements from a nearby university taught the class and thereby minimized the effect of a consistent program.

Inconsistent teaching creates tensions and suspicions in the students. The children are not sure where they stand or what is going to happen next. They need a more secure environment in order to learn.

Irrelevant materials, outmoded lessons, and all kinds of busy work rob students of a chance to learn. Given a good environment, proper materials, adequate motivation, and lots of encouragement, the students' innate curiosities and desire to learn take over and they will teach themselves.

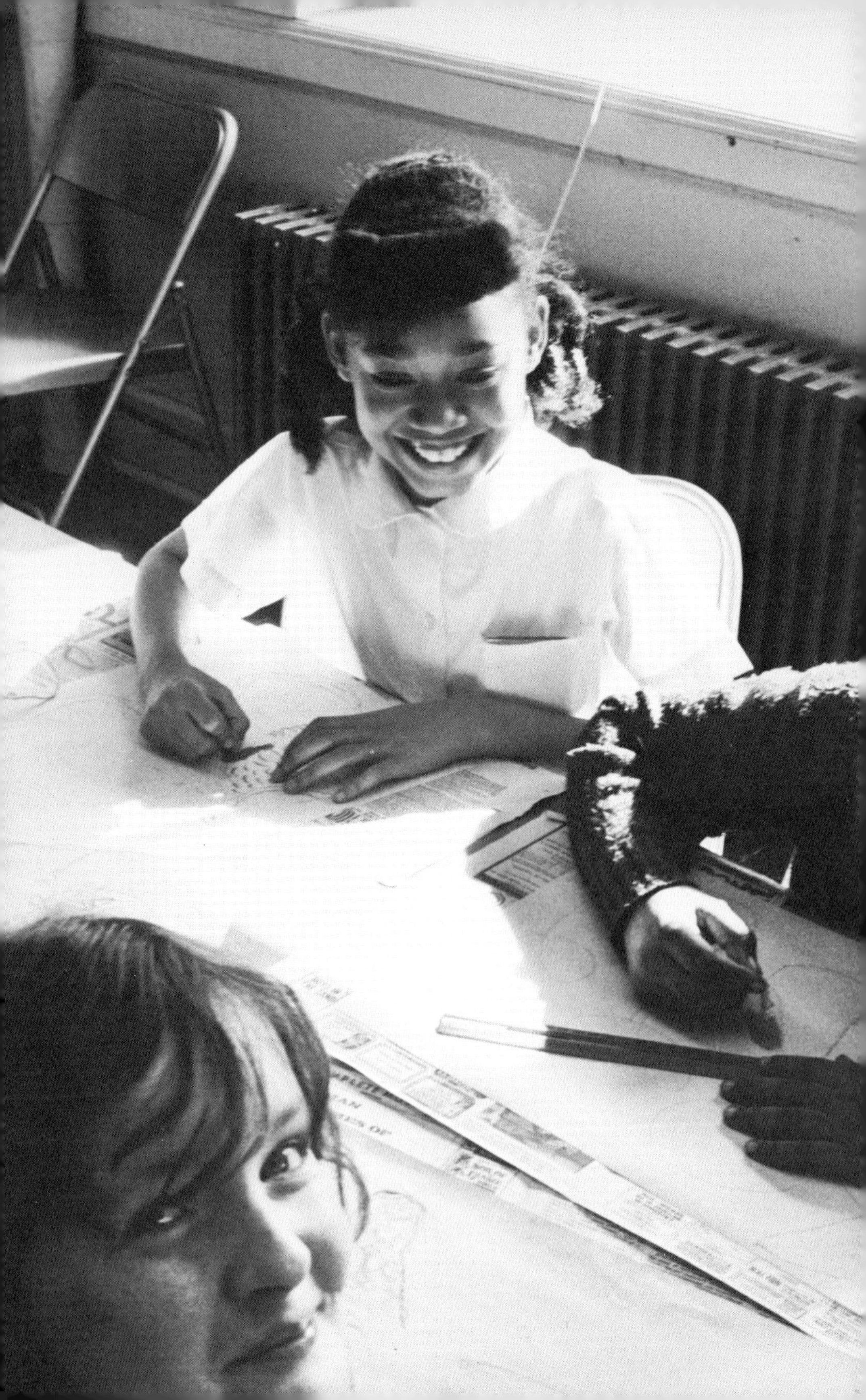

B

Cross-level Tutoring

If a teacher tries to give the same assignment to a widely diversified group of students, there is sure to be trouble. One solution to this problem is more individualized instruction and perhaps a cross-level tutoring program.

At St. Bride School in Chicago a cross-level tutoring program was arranged for certain sixth grade students who were deficient in reading and math skills. Their average reading level was about 2.1. These girls and boys were trained to tutor younger children in the primary grade levels.

The older students had been humiliated by attempts to teach them second grade material. However, with the incentive of being tutors they learned the skills in which they were deficient and learned them very rapidly. The younger children also gained remarkably in the one-to-one relationship. Most of the help given the primary children was in the form of word recognition skills. Many were unsure of their consonant and vowel sounds. None were proficient at reading the vocabulary words at their own reading levels. The older students would be taught the same lesson they were to teach the younger children. With all the practice in phonetics, the older children's work improved steadily. One teacher told me that interest in school work had picked up. One boy received 100 percent on his spelling tests, whereas his highest score before he began tutoring was 30 percent.

Tokens were used with these two groups in a unique way. Each tutor was given ten tokens each day to distribute to his "student." The tutors were instructed to use much verbal praise and to give the tokens one at a time when the child worked hard for a total of five minutes. The younger child was also given tokens for his tutor, three of them. These were to be given to the tutor at the end of the class period. Three if the child felt happy because the tutor had been nice to him. Two tokens if the tutor was pretty good, but not the best. One token if the child felt that his tutor could have done better.

The tokens could be spent immediately after the tutoring period in ten minutes of free time in a recreation room where TV and games were available. On Friday, because of scheduling difficulties, the recreation room was not available, but the children could spend their tokens for candy or books or some type of novelty.

I was present for all the tutoring sessions and I learned of only one instance of extortion. A young child came and told me his tutor said that if he didn't give him three tokens he'd get beaten up. The sixth grader was dismissed from the tutoring corps with an explanation so that he knew why. The problem did not come up again. Being a tutor had a certain prestige to it; it allowed the tutor to be out of class for an hour each day. The class missed was the reading class. In tutoring they were learning basic skills which were needed for their own more difficult reading assignments.

A teacher's chief aim should be to arrange the conditions and environments so that learning can take place. If students find it more profitable and enjoyable to study than not to study, they will study eagerly. But if there are no apparent rewards, motivation is low, and students will do as little as possible to get by.

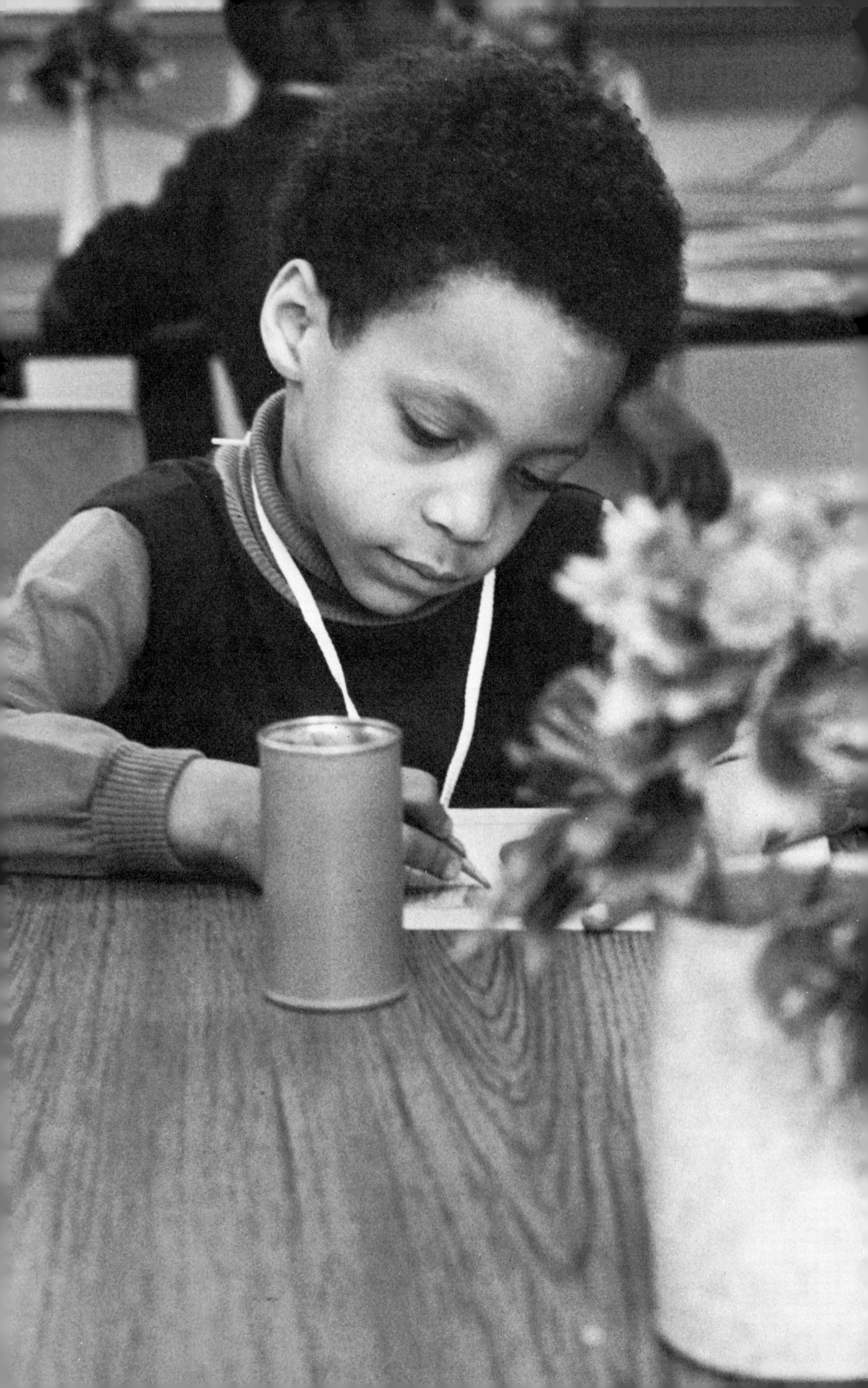

bibliography

This brief list of books which follows is simply provided to indicate some of the related and more technical literature available to the teacher who wishes to learn more about behavior analysis and behavior modification in the classroom.

Becker, Wesley C., Engelmann, Siegfried, and Thomas, Don R., _Teaching: A Course in Applied Psychology_. Chicago: Science Research Associates, Inc., 1971. Paper, 466 pages. Bibliography.

Blackham, G. and Silberman, A., _Modification of Child Behavior: Principles and Procedures_. Belmont, California: Wadsworth Publishing Company, Inc., 1970. 186 pages. Bibliography.

Blackwood, Ralph O., <u>Operant Control of Behavior</u>: <u>Elimination of Misbehavior and Motivation of Children</u>. Akron, Ohio: Exordium Press, 1971. 240 pages. Bibliography.

Buckley, Nancy K., and Walker, Hill M., <u>Modifying Classroom Behavior</u>: <u>A Manual of Procedure for Classroom Teachers</u>. Champaign, Illinois: Research Press, 1970. Paper, 124 pages.

Bushell, Jr., Don, <u>Classroom Behavior</u>: <u>A Little Book for Teachers</u>. Englewood Cliffs, New Jersey: Prentiss-Hall, Inc., 1973. Paper, 131 pages. Bibliography.

Carter, Ronald D.., <u>Help, These Kids Are Driving Me Crazy</u>. Champaign, Illinois: Research Press, 1972. Paper, 112 pages.

Fargo, George A., Behrns, Charlene, and Nolen, Patricia, <u>Behavior Modification in the Classroom</u>. Belmont, California: Wadsworth Publishing Co., 1970. Paper, 344 pages.

Hamblin, Robert L., Buckholdt, David, Ferritor, Daniel, Kozloff, Martin, and Blackwell, Lois, <u>The Humanization Processes</u>: <u>A Social, Behavioral Analysis of Childrens' Problems</u>. New York: John Wiley & Sons, Inc., 1971. 286 pages. Bibliography.

Harris, Mary B., ed., <u>Classroom Uses of Behavior Modification</u>. Columbus, Ohio: Charles E. Merrill Publishing Co., 1972. Paper, 433 pages.

Homme, Lloyd, Csanyi, Attila P., Gonzales, Mary Ann, and Rechs, James R., <u>How To Use Contingency Contracting in the Classroom</u>. Champaign, Illinois: Research Press, Inc., 1970. Paper, 130 pages.

Madsen, Charles H., Jr., and Madsen, Clifford K., <u>Teaching/Discipline: Behavioral Principles Toward a Positive Approach</u>. Boston: Allyn & Bacon, Inc., 1970. 136 pages. Bibliography.

Meacham, Merle L., and Wiesen, Allen E., <u>Changing Classroom Behavior, A Manual for Precision Teaching</u>. Scranton, Pennsylvania: International Textbook Company, 1969. Paper, 212 pages. Bibliography.

O'Leary, K. Daniel, and O'Leary, Susan G., eds., <u>Classroom Management: The Successful Use of Behavior Modification</u>. New York: Pergamon Press, Inc., 1972. 664 pages. Bibliography.

Sarason, Irwin G., Glaser, Edward M., and Fargo, George A., <u>Reinforcing Productive Classroom Behavior</u>. New York: Behavioral Publications, 1972. Paper, 43 pages.

Sheppard, William C., Shank, Steven B., and Wilson, Darla, <u>How To Be A Good Teacher: Training Social Behavior in Young Children</u>. Champaign, Illinois: Research Press Co., 1972. Paper, 94 pages.

Skinner, B. F., <u>The Technology of Teaching</u>. New York: Appleton-Century-Crofts, 1968. Paper, 264 pages.

Sulzer, Beth, and Mayer, Roy G., *Behavior Modification Procedures for School Personnel*. Hinsdale, Illinois: The Dryden Press, 1972. Paper, 316 pages.

notes